How to Pass
Advanced
Numeracy
Tests

More titles in the Testing series:

www.koganpage.com

KoganPage

How to Pass
Advanced Numeracy Tests

Improve your scores in numerical reasoning and data interpretation psychometric tests

Mike Bryon
Second edition

KoganPage

LONDON PHILADELPHIA NEW DELHI

6054556

First published in 2002 by Kogan Page Limited
Revised edition 2008
Second edition 2010
Reissued 2013
Reprinted 2013

120 Pentonville Road	1518 Walnut Street, Suite 1100	4737/23 Ansari Road
London N1 9JN	Philadelphia PA 19102	Daryaganj
United Kingdom	USA	New Delhi 110002
www.koganpage.com		India

© Mike Bryon 2002, 2008, 2010, 2013

ISBN   978 0 7494 6789 0
E-ISBN 978 0 7494 6790 6

British Library Cataloguing-in-Publication Data

A CIP record for this book is available from the British Library.

The Library of Congress has already cataloged the previous issue as follows:

Bryon, Mike.
  How to pass advanced numeracy tests : improve your scores in numerical reasoning and data interpretation psychometric tests / Mike Bryon. – 2nd ed.
    p. cm.
    ISBN 978-0-7494-6081-5 – ISBN 978-0-7494-6082-2   1. Verbal ability–Testing.
2. English language–Usage–Testing.   3. Reasoning (Psychology)–Testing.
4. Reading comprehension–Ability testing.   I. Title.
    BF463.V45B79 2010
    510.76–dc22   2010016042

Typeset by Graphicraft Limited, Hong Kong
Printed and bound in Great Britain by Ashford Colour Press Ltd, Gosport, Hants

Contents

Acknowledgements

I owe thanks to Carla Valerio-Chapperon, Miriam Walfisz and Ed Hateley for contributing many practice questions and checking answers. Their contributions make the title a far better book and I trust more valuable as a source of practice. The views expressed and any errors are entirely my own.

Mike Bryon – A pioneer in test coaching

Employers used to argue that candidates could not improve their score in psychometric tests. Mike Bryon proved otherwise. It is now unanimously acknowledged that every candidate can improve how they perform in these common selection tools.

Mike Bryon was first published in 1991 and now has 17 books in print on how to pass the tests and assessments used by large employers. He is the best selling author on the subject. Each book contains advice on the winning mind set, insights and tips, hundreds of realistic example questions, practice tests, answers, explanations and interpretations of your score. Hundreds of thousands of people have used the books to get down to some serious score improving practice and succeed in the test and assessments they face. The books have sold worldwide and have been translated into many foreign languages including Indonesian, Portuguese, Russian, Polish, Indian and Chinese.

After three years of postgraduate research into adult learning at the University of Birmingham (UK) he founded a consultancy, and for 15 years he provided recruitment and diversity consultancy to organizations in every industrial sector and a great many major UK and international companies, including Departments of the UK Government, National utilities, high street retail chains, rail companies, local and emergency authorities, and multinationals such as the Ford Motor Company and British Airport Authorities. The consultancy contributed extensively to EU research programmes with research partners drawn from across the union.

His books review the strategies and provide the practice you need to gain a competitive advantage. Importantly they offer practice at a level that reflects that of the actual tests. These books really do offer hundreds of realistic practice questions; 400 or 500 as a minimum. Many of the titles offer far more than this. *The Ultimate Psychometric Test Book* contains over 1,000 practice questions and is perfect for the candidate who faces tests at the intermediate level or seeks an introduction to graduate material.

The titles reach across the whole testing spectrum from inter-mediate through to graduate and the high flyer. There is winning advice, insights and tips on personality questionnaires, situational awareness tests, assessment days, group exercises, role plays and in-tray or e-tray exercises. There are books to help candidates who dare to dream of a single career goal including applicant firefight-ers, candidates for the UK civil service (including the FastStream), postgraduate business schools applicants who face the GMAT and medical school applicants who face the UKCAT. Mike Bryon has also written on secondary transfer for children of 11 years of age, and adults who face a test as speakers of English as a second language.

Mike Bryon has over 10 years of experience in the training room, making sure every candidate demonstrates their full potential and realizes the career of their choice. His ground-breaking approach has proved decisive for countless thousands of candidates.

His work remains contemporary through his continual research and writing and through the many readers who contact him for advice and suggestions on sources of practice questions. During your programme of review, if you hit a problem or if you would like suggestions of sources of practice material then e-mail Mike Bryon at: help@mikebryon.com.

Part One
Psychometric
tests and practice

Chapter 1
Demonstrate your true potential

How this book will help

This book provides highly relevant practice questions and explanations that will help candidates prepare for psychometric tests of numerical skills. It deals extensively with the core competencies tested at the advanced level including: analytical skills in a financial context; the comprehension of financial language; the ability to discover data relevant to financial decisions; decision making with numerical data; the ability to learn and apply numerical ratios and solve business problems. It also reviews the numerical methods and rules that underlie psychometric tests of numerical skills.

Many readers of the existing Kogan Page list of testing books have requested more practice numerical questions and more challenging material than is currently available. In response, this title offers many hundreds of new questions, including four realistic mock tests relevant to numerical skills tests used by employers and educational institutions today.

Like a real test, each chapter starts with easier questions that get progressively harder. Again, in response to readers' requests, many more detailed explanations to answers have been provided.

The challenge of numerical tests

Employers' numerical tests represent a considerable challenge to candidates who have specialized in numerical disciplines, let alone those who have not. Often accomplished individuals may not have practised their numerical skills for some years and need to revise them if they are to present themselves as the all-round candidate who possesses both numerical and verbal competencies.

Even if you feel confident with your numerical skills, these exercises will help you to achieve, as psychometric tests are used to recruit to many top jobs, careers and professions and there is considerable competition amongst many candidates. You have to be at your very best if you are to succeed in your chosen career, and only practice will ensure that you maximize the advantage you enjoy over others.

What are psychometric tests?

The user of this book is likely to face a psychometric test in relation to their work or study. Many readers will have applied for a job or course of study and found that the process involves them taking a test. In this context psychometric tests are used by the institution or employer for selection purposes.

The tests comprise a standardized series of problems, either multiple choice or short-answer, taken with either pen and paper, at a computer terminal or, increasingly, online. The conditions under which the test is taken will be the same for everyone. Strict time limits are likely to apply and the results will be marked or scored in a way that allows comparisons to be drawn between candidates. At the graduate and professional end of the testing spectrum they are likely to be tests of endurance lasting many hours. They comprise a series or battery of tests sat one after the other. It is therefore all the more important for candidates to adopt strategies to maximize their score.

What to expect on the day

Think back to the days of examinations at school or university. You will attend a test centre with a room set out either as an examination hall with small desks or with banks of computer terminals, depending on whether you face a paper and pen or computer administered version of the test.

Other candidates are very likely to be present. In some instances there may be many other candidates. A test administrator will welcome you and explain the process. He or she will be following a prepared script and will be happy to answer any questions that you may have, although the answers given may seem rather brief or superficial. The administrator will be reluctant to stray far from the script so that all candidates (including those who have attended on other days and will not have heard your question) receive the same information and experience the same test conditions.

If you suffer a disability that may affect your performance in the test or that requires you to sit the test under different circumstances, contact the organization that has invited you straightaway.

Interpreting your score

The scoring of tests is quite complex and individuals responsible for the interpretation of results should be trained to a level recommended by the British Psychological Society. Scoring involves comparing a candidate's score against the scores of a sample of the wider population with broadly similar backgrounds. Unsurprisingly, there is a tendency among recruiters to assume that the higher a candidate scores, the greater the candidate's likely performance in the job. Equally common is the tendency for the recruiter to be relieved that poor-scoring candidates, whom the test predicts will not perform well in the job, have been identified in such a clear-cut way.

However, doing well or badly in a test does not necessarily mean that you have or do not have the potential to perform well in a particular job. Tests are at best only indicators of potential. Had you been less nervous or better prepared on the day of the test then you might have realized a considerably different score and been classified quite differently. Performance in the majority of jobs is a difficult thing to define and is influenced by a wide range of factors. The occupational psychologist must attribute to the job in question a single set of criteria against which to assess performance, and this risks attributing to the workplace too simplistic a model of what makes someone good at his or her job.

If you fail a test it does not mean that you do not have the potential to do the job or pursue the career. You may be perfectly able to do the job and indeed would pass the test if you took it again. Ask the organization to provide you with feedback on your score. Some organizations are happy to do this and their comments will help you to identify any areas in which you need to improve. Try to recall and note down the types of question and the level of difficulty. Plan a new programme of practice and concentrate your efforts on improving your skills in the areas in which you did least well.

Hundreds more practice questions and tests are available in the companion title *The Advanced Numeracy Test Workbook*. Additional advance material is also available in the *Graduate Psychometric Test Workbook*. Both titles are published by Kogan Page.

Chapter 2
The winning approach

The ability to do well in a test is not some innate quality over which you have no influence. Your score is to a large extent dependent on your approach on the day and the degree to which you are prepared for the challenge.

How you approach a test is critical to success. It is important that you treat it as an opportunity to demonstrate your true potential. Avoid feelings of resentment or a fear of failure whereby you commit less than your full worth. If passing the test means that you can realize a life goal then you have every reason to try your best and attend fully prepared.

Studies have shown that the difference between the soloist in an orchestra, the top athlete or chess grandmaster and the rest is often down to practice, practice, practice. The key is to stretch yourself and not simply repeat tasks you can already do easily. Practice before a test is essential and can make a significant difference to your performance. Practice makes a difference in many types of test, including numerical tests. It is obvious that practice will help because it means you are likely to make fewer mistakes and are faster against the often-tight time constraints. Importantly, practice allows you to revise forgotten rules and develop a good test technique. This involves becoming familiar with the format of the questions and maximizing your score through, for example, educated guessing.

Remember, when used as a part of a selection process you should treat a psychometric test like a competition in which you *must* do better than other candidates. If passing the test is important then you should be prepared to make a major commitment in terms of practice before the real test, starting as soon as possible. Other candidates will make such a commitment and if you don't, you risk coming a poor second.

Key stages to a winning approach

Under the two headings 'Work harder' and 'Work smarter' below, there are eight sections offering advice and tips on the best approach to adopt when preparing for a psychometric test.

Work harder

Make time for practice

Given that you use your time sensibly and that you work in a way which reduces your weaknesses and maximizes your strengths, the amount of time you can devote to intelligent, directed practice will be crucial. You have already decided that this test is important to you, so you need to make sure you find time to do yourself justice and to demonstrate your potential. Those who succeed are often those with the greatest desire, the greatest tenacity.

Start your practice as soon as you suspect you might have a test (though you should make sure you are working on the right kind of exercise – see 'Work smarter' below).

Work smarter

Decide how to practise

Everyone can improve his or her test score with practice and the more you practise something you find challenging the better you will do. However, the optimum amount of practice depends on your starting point. For example, the candidate who is otherwise likely to fail by only a few marks stands to gain a lot very quickly because a little practice is almost certain to mean that they pass something they would otherwise have failed. Someone who has not used their numerical skills for some years will need to relearn the rules and regain their lost speed and accuracy before they can demonstrate their true potential. This may require a quite considerable commitment. A candidate who never got on with maths or science at school and specialized at university in an arts subject may need to commit many weeks of effort to master skills they had previously managed without. Be clear about what you need to practise and make time to do it.

Start your programme of practice in good time

Try to place yourself somewhere on a scale between reasonably confident and someone whose numerical skills are very rusty. If you fall within these bounds then the amount of practice you need to undertake is likely to lie between a minimum of 12 hours and putting aside a few hours a day for three or four weeks.

It is best to practise up to the day before the test. But try to leave yourself a little scope in case you underestimate the challenge and need more time than you initially allowed.

Be clear as to the type of test you face

Improvements in scores are obtained by practising on material similar to that which occurs in the real test. It is essential, therefore, that you establish the types of question you face and find material as similar as possible. The organization might have sent you a description of the test or have a website that contains a number of sample questions. If this is not the case, call them and request a description of the test and as much information as possible. Every bit of information helps, so try requesting a verbal description over the telephone or simply ask them to list the titles of the sub-tests that make up the battery and the name of the publisher. Establish if the test is administered with paper and pen or at a computer terminal, for how long you need to attend and whether or not a calculator is provided. Be aware of the fact that sample questions are usually less difficult examples of the type of question contained in the real test.

Plan to undertake two sorts of practice:

1 Practice without time constraint and in an informal relaxed situation. The aim of this sort of practice is that you realize the demands of the questions and the mathematical principles behind them and build up your confidence. It is fine to work collaboratively with someone who also faces the test or a mentor willing to help.

  If your maths is weak or rusty then this type of practice will form the bulk of your efforts. Make sure that you practise both on realistic questions and on the content of some of the very good revision study guides and textbooks that are available for GCSE and A-level students, for example.

2 Practice with realistic questions against a strict time constraint and under realistic test-like conditions. The aim of these 'mock tests' is to get used to answering the questions under the type of conditions that will exist when you take the real test. This type of question helps you to avoid mistakes when under pressure and to develop a good test strategy. You should aim to take a minimum of four mock tests.

  It is important to get the right balance between speed and accuracy as more correct answers will give you a higher score, but you may well be penalized for giving incorrect answers or no answers.

Collect appropriate practice material

Do not spend time or money on material that is *not* similar to the real questions in the test that you face. The content of the book should contain material that is relevant to any numerical part of the test. Further material is available from the list of Kogan Page testing titles at the back of this volume.

Concentrate on your personal challenges

We all like to spend time on things at which we excel. But when practising for a test it is essential that you focus most of your efforts on improving your areas of weakness. This may require a degree of courage and a critical review of your strengths and weaknesses. If you have always been less good at maths, now is the time to put this situation right.

It may prove boring, painful even, but a programme of revision and practice under test-like conditions will afford you the speed, accuracy and skills to do well in employers' numerical tests. Give yourself sufficient time to succeed and don't give up or shy away from asking for help; don't fool yourself that you understand something if you don't. Keep going over explanations and examples until you understand the principle fully, and then keep practising at realistic questions until you are confident and accurate. Try working with a variety of texts that are all likely to offer slightly different explanations. Libraries and bookshops stock an extensive range of revision and study books on, for example, mathematics and business studies that explain well the key principles examined by these tests.

Your practice should aim to make sure that you are confident in all aspects of the tests, including strategies for maximizing your score, covered in the next section.

Adopt the very best of test strategies

The best-scoring candidates arrive very well prepared. You should attend on the day of your test fully aware of the demands. Before the start of the test, the test administrator or computer program will allow you to review a number of sample questions and go over the amount of time allowed. All this information should be entirely familiar and your programme of practice should have covered all the types of question described.

The top-scoring candidates are the ones who look forward to the test as an opportunity to demonstrate their abilities. They have confidence in themselves and preparation is key to confidence. They realize that they have nothing to lose if they do their best and 'go for it'.

It is important to organize your time during the test. Keep a check on how long you spend on any one question and keep going right up to the end. You have to get right a balance between speed and accuracy. This again is something that takes practice, especially as you may well suffer anxiety during the real test and therefore be prone to making more mistakes.

Estimating answers and modifying sums to more convenient figures so that calculations are faster sometimes pays. You can then look at the suggested answers and pick out the correct one.

You will get some answers wrong. It is better that you attempt every question and risk getting some wrong than check every answer twice, only to be told that you have run out of time.

If you find a series of difficult questions – keep going. The next section may comprise something at which you excel, so never give up, just move on.

Simply guessing at answers is unlikely to help. This is because many tests penalize wrong answers or unanswered questions. If you cannot answer a question it is far better to guess in an educated manner. This involves looking at the suggested answers and attempting to rule some of them out as definitely wrong. You then guess from the remaining options and hopefully increase your chances of guessing correctly.

Practise managing your time in a way that ensures you have enough time to attempt every question and apply educated guessing to any questions you cannot answer.

Make best use of this book

At the time of going to print I believe the material in this book will help you revise the numerical skills examined by tests currently used by major employers and provide you with many hours' worth of relevant practice questions. These tests include, for example, the ABLE Financial Appraisal Exercise, the McKinsey Problem Solving Test, the GMAT and SHL graduate battery to name a few. But, as with any study aid, before you invest time or money in using the book, make sure the material within it is in fact relevant to the particular challenge that you face.

When you practise on these questions, try not to use a calculator. In some tests a calculator is provided but you need to be able to see that the answer you get using a calculator is broadly correct, so practice at manually working out the sums is still essential.

If you are having problems finding practice material that is similar to or as difficult as the test you have to take, then by all means contact me at help@mikebryon.com and if I know of any other sources I will be glad to let you know. Please note that you will need to give me a clear idea of the type of test you face.

I apologize in advance if you discover an error in these practice questions; try not to allow it to undermine your confidence in the value of practice; and try not to take too dim a view of this book because it most definitely does contain valuable practice material. I have made every effort to identify all the mistakes that somehow creep into a text of this kind and I hope I have not missed too many. I will be glad to hear of any that I have missed in order that mistakes can be removed at the next reprint.

Part Two
Hundreds of really relevant practice questions

Chapter 3
Quantitative reasoning

Tests start easy and get harder so make sure that you get all the available early marks and complete the relatively easy section in the minimum time. This will place you at a considerable advantage in terms of having both maximum time to tackle the rest of the test, and an unbeatable initial score on which to build a winning performance.

This chapter reviews the methods and rules that underlie many psychometric tests of numerical skills. Use it to build up speed and confidence and revise the basics. Answers and many detailed explanations are found in Part Three. Be sure that you work out these sums manually if you face a test in which a calculator is not allowed.

Practice questions – revise the basics

At the intermediate level a very common test question involves the conversion of currencies. Use the information provided in the table to answer the first three questions.

Currency exchange

1 USD =	88.25 JPY
1 EUR =	1.47 USD
1 GBP =	11.82 ZAR
1 AUD =	0.97 USD
1 RUB =	0.022 EUR

1 How many JPY are equivalent to
40 USD? *Answer*

2 What value in EUR's are equivalent
to 200 RUB? *Answer*

3 Which suggested answer is the closest inverse exchange rate
for GBP = ZAR

A 1 ZAR: 0.0845 GBP

B 1 ZAR: 0.0846 GBP

C 1 ZAR: 0.0847 GBP

D 1 ZAR: 0.0848 GBP

Answer

4 Complete the following conversions between fractions, decimals and percentages:

$\frac{1}{2}$		
	0.75	
		20%
$\frac{3}{5}$		
		37.5%
	0.25	

5   Which of the definitions is the meaning of median?

   A Most common answer

   B The range from smallest to biggest

   C The middle number

   Answer [   ]

6   If W is an integer, what does
        $50 \leq W < 100$ mean?   *Answer* [   ]

7   What does the $\leq$ symbol mean?

                                Answer [   ]

8   What does the $<$ symbol mean?

                                Answer [   ]

9   What does the $>$ symbol mean?

                                Answer [   ]

10   Which of the four statements best describes the scatter graph?

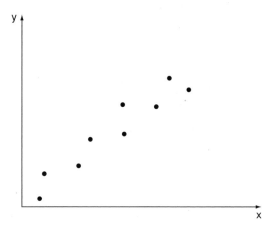

   A Strong negative correlation

   B Poor correlation

C Reasonable positive correlation

D Reasonable negative correlation

Answer [   ]

11 A bag contains six yellow discs, five white and nine black. If one disc is selected, what is the probability of it being black?

Answer [   ]

12 What is the chance of not getting a black disc?

Answer [   ]

13 Express 9/20 as a percentage and a decimal.

Answer [   ]

14 For the following set of numbers find the mean:

2   6   9   13   14   19

Answer [   ]

15 For the following set of numbers find the median and range:

2   6   9   13   14   19

Answer

Median [   ]

Range [   ]

16 Which of the following numbers would be included in the group $20 \le x < 70$?

A   B   C   D

35   72   19   30

Answer [   ]

17 List all the possible outcomes if you were to toss two coins.   *Answer* [   ]

18   If you were to toss a coin and roll a six-sided dice, what is the probability of getting a head and a 1?

Answer [　　　　　　　]

19   'Congruent' means:

A	B	C	D
The same	The same size	The same shape	Similar

Answer [　　　　　　　]

20   Which of the following is a type of transformation?

A	B	C
Translation	Enlargement	Rotation

D	E
Reflection	All of these

Answer [　　　　　　　]

21   What is 3 to the power of 6?

Answer [　　　　　　　]

22   What is 4 cubed?

Answer [　　　　　　　]

23   What power of 2 makes 16?

Answer [　　　　　　　]

24   A square has an area of 25 m².
What is the length of its sides?   *Answer* [　　　　　　　]

25   Which of the following formulas describes the relationship between the diameter and radius of a circle?

A	B	C
$d = 2r$	$d = \pi r$	$d = 2/r$

Answer [　　　　　　　]

26 As a decimal π is approximated as 3.142. What is this as a fraction?

Answer _____

27 Angles in mathematics can be either positive or negative. Which of the angles illustrated is positive?

C–A   C–B

Answer _____

28 How many common factors does the number 32 have (include trivial factors)?

A   B   C   D   E   F
1   2   3   4   5   6

Answer _____

29 What is the highest common factor of 24 and 32?   Answer _____

30 What are the common factors of 13?

Answer _____

31 The common factors of 19 are 1 and 19 only. What does this make 19?

Answer _____

32 How many of the following are prime numbers?
4, 5, 7, 12, 17   Answer _____

33   How many common factors has 48 (exclude the trivial factors)?

A   B   C   D   E
5   6   7   8   9

Answer [   ]

34   Find the highest common factor of 18 and 54.

Answer [   ]

35   What does 2^3 equal?

A   B   C   D   E
4   5   6   7   8

Answer [   ]

36   What does 2 to the power of 5 equal?

Answer [   ]

37   What does 3 to the power of 4 equal?

Answer [   ]

38   3 to the power of 4 divided by 3 to the power of 2 is the same as:

A 13 divided by 6

B 81 divided by 9

C 27 divided by 6

D 27 divided by 9

Answer [   ]

39   16 × 32 is the same as:

A 2 to the power of 8 × 2 to the power of 16

B 2 to the power of 3 × 2 to the power of 4

C 2 to the power of 4 × 2 to the power of 5

D 3 to the power of 6 × 2 to the power of 7

Answer [   ]

40 If the radius of the earth is 6,378 km, what is the circumference?

Answer ⬚

41 Convert the following percentages into decimals:

5% _____

17.5% _____

25% _____

150% _____

0.5% _____

42 Find 117 as a percentage of 565.

Answer ⬚

43 Find 126 as a percentage of 360.

Answer ⬚

44 Find 272 as a percentage of 680.

Answer ⬚

45 Find 56 and 42 as a percentage of 280.

Answer ⬚

46 Find 301 as a percentage of 430.

Answer ⬚

47 Increase 90 by 17.5%.

Answer ⬚

48 Increase 85 by 15%.

Answer ⬚

49 Increase 15 by 60%.

Answer

50 Decrease 140 by 24%.

Answer

51 Decrease 63 by 20%.

Answer

52 Decrease 73 by 82%.

Answer

53 What amount when increased by 20% gives 300?

Answer

54 What amount when increased by 12% gives 420?

Answer

55 What amount when increased by 50% gives 645?

Answer

56 Simplify 40:240.

Answer

57 Simplify 60:390.

Answer

58 Simplify 75:350.

Answer

59 Simplify 9:63.

Answer

60 Simplify 95:247.

Answer

61 Divide 63 into the ratio of 3:6.

Answer ⬚

62 Divide 132 into the ratio of 2:3:1.

Answer ⬚

63 Divide £12.00 into the ratio 9:7:8.

Answer ⬚

64 Find the value of x:

$3x - 3 = 18$

Answer ⬚

65 Find the value of x:

$5(x + 6) = 75$

Answer ⬚

66 Find the value of x:

$6x + 10 = 3x - 6$

Answer ⬚

67 Find the value of x:

$2(x + 9) = 3(2x - 3)$

Answer ⬚

68 Find the value of x:

$1/2(x + 2) = 1/8(3x + 4)$

Answer ⬚

69 Why are these types of equations called linear equations?

Answer ⬚

70 Which equation corresponds to this graph?

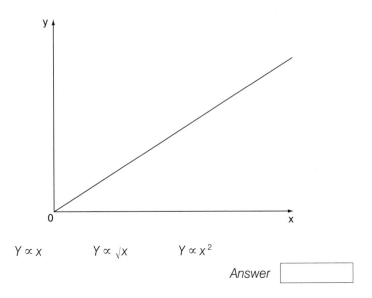

$Y \propto x$ $\qquad$ $Y \propto \sqrt{x}$ $\qquad$ $Y \propto x^2$

Answer ☐

71 Which equation corresponds to this graph?

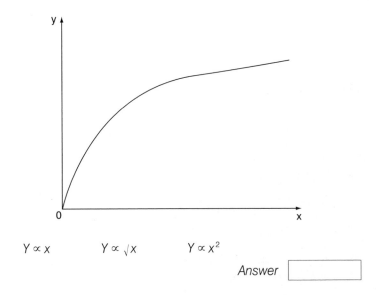

$Y \propto x$ $\qquad$ $Y \propto \sqrt{x}$ $\qquad$ $Y \propto x^2$

Answer ☐

72 Which equation corresponds to this graph?

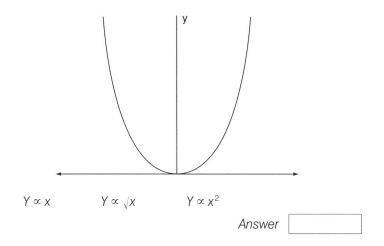

$Y \propto x$ $\qquad$ $Y \propto \sqrt{x}$ $\qquad$ $Y \propto x^2$

Answer [   ]

73 Interpret the following graph to answer the questions:

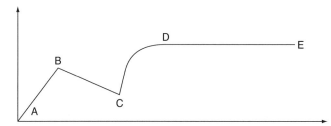

Between what points is the object stationary?

A	B	C	D
A–B	B–C	C–D	D–E

When is the object's distance increasing steadily?

A	B	C	D
A–B	B–C	C–D	D–E

When is the object going back on itself?

A	B	C	D
A–B	B–C	C–D	D–E

Answer [   ]

74   To estimate the number of commuters who cycle to work, 30 randomly selected cyclists a day are stopped over five days. On average three cyclists per day are found to have taken part in the survey before. Estimate the total population of cyclists.

Answer [   ]

75   A culture of bacteria grows by a ratio of 1:2 every two hours. Describe the size of the culture after 10 hours.

Answer [   ]

76   A currency is devalued by a factor of 0.02 a year. What percentage of its original value will it have after four years? Express your answer to the nearest full percentage.

Answer [   ]

77   A 1 kg block of ice is melting by 9/10th of its mass each hour. What will be its mass after three hours?

A   B   C   D
100 gm   10 gm   1 gm   0.1 gm

Answer [   ]

78   A town with a population of 2,000 is expected to increase by 30 per cent per annum. What will its population be in four years' time?

Answer [   ]

79   A customer base of 1,500 has grown by a factor of 0.08 each year. For how many years must this rate of growth continue in order that the customer base exceeds 2,000 clients?

Answer [   ]

From the following frequency table, answer the questions that follow:

5					5	5	6	7	
6			3	4	4	5	5		
7		2	3	4	4	5			9
8	0								
9									
10									

80 Which group has the highest frequency?

Answer

81 What is the median result?

Answer

82 Find the three-point moving average for the following data points (express your answer to the nearest decimal point).

Answer

83 A sample of 200 must be proportional to the total, which comprises:

Yellow shirts	1,500
Blue shirts	2,000
Red shirts	500

What would be a proportionally representative sample?

Answer

84 Which of the two measures of variation would you use to analyse data that had a distinct positive skew?

1. Standard deviation

2. Inter-quartile range

Answer [ ]

85 A bag contains 20 balls, 10 of which are white and 10 black. What are the odds of drawing two black balls one after the other? Assume that the first black ball is replaced after it is drawn.

A	B	C	D
1 in 3	1 in 2	1 in 4	1 in 8

Answer [ ]

86 A bag contains 20 white balls. The probability that three white balls are drawn is:

A	B	C	D
0.5	100	1	3/20

Answer [ ]

87 Calculate the surface area of this shape:

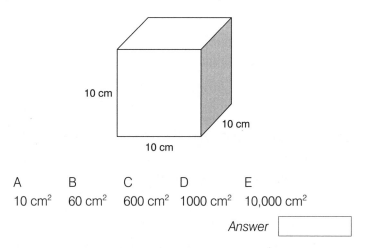

10 cm
10 cm
10 cm

A	B	C	D	E
10 cm²	60 cm²	600 cm²	1000 cm²	10,000 cm²

Answer [ ]

88 Solve the following equation:

$(4^2 - 3^2) - 2^4 =$

A	B	C	D	E
8	9	10	17	23

Answer

89 What is the volume of this shape?

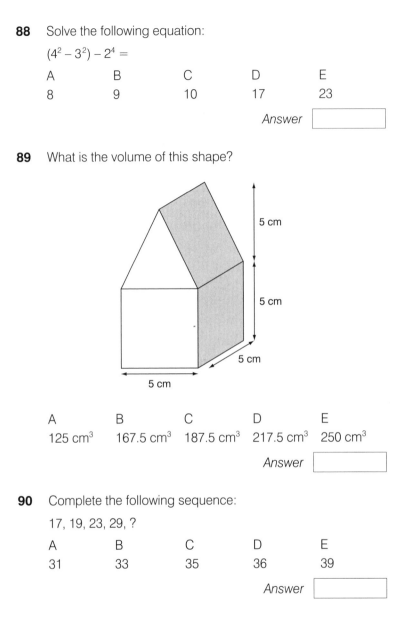

5 cm

5 cm

5 cm

5 cm

A	B	C	D	E
125 cm³	167.5 cm³	187.5 cm³	217.5 cm³	250 cm³

Answer

90 Complete the following sequence:

17, 19, 23, 29, ?

A	B	C	D	E
31	33	35	36	39

Answer

91   Solve the following equation:

$$\frac{4x^3}{x^2}$$

A	B	C	D	E
4	$4x$	$4x^2$	x^2	16

Answer [   ]

92   Solve the following:

20% of all trains are cancelled

20% of trains that run break down

Out of the trains that are not cancelled and do not break down, one-quarter arrive late

What percentage of all trains arrive on time?

A	B	C	D	E
40%	45%	48%	54%	60%

Answer [   ]

93   What is the value of x in this sequence?

1, 3, ?, x, ?, 21, 28

A	B	C	D	E
7	9	10	13	17

Answer [   ]

94   There are six times as many red blocks as there are green blocks. There are twice as many blue blocks as there are red blocks. What is the ratio of blue blocks to green blocks?

A	B	C	D	E
6:2	2:1	3:1	1:3	12:1

Answer [   ]

95   Compound interest is calculated on a loan at a rate of 10 per cent per annum. Assuming no repayments are made, how much will be owed after three years on a £10,000 loan?

A	B	C	D	E
£12,000	£13,000	£13,100	£13,300	£13,310

Answer [   ]

96   A barrel containing 200 l of water leaks at a rate of 500 cl per day. How many days will it take for the barrel to empty?

A	B	C	D	E
4	25	40	250	400

Answer [   ]

97   Out of 2,000 companies, 180 will cease trading in a given year. What is this expressed as a percentage?

A	B	C	D	E
4.5%	6%	9%	12%	15%

Answer [   ]

98   How much carpet do I need to cover one room which is 12 m × 18 m and a second room which is 15 m × 15 m?

A	B	C	D	E
60 m²	360 m²	441 m²	541 m²	675 m²

Answer [   ]

99   How many metres cubed of water are there in a full swimming pool which is 25 m long, 12 m wide and has an average depth of 6 m?

A	B	C	D	E
180	900	2,700	1,800	36,000

Answer [   ]

100 In a team game the total score for all 22 players was 462. What was the average (mean) score?

A	B	C	D	E
17	18	19	20	21

Answer [ ]

101 A salesperson needs to generate £5,000 profit for the company each month. She sells two products. On product A she makes 25 per cent, on product B she makes 40 per cent profit. If she sold £12,000 worth of product A in a given month, what value of product B must she sell to reach the target?

A	B	C	D	E
£5,000	£7,500	£8,200	£9,000	£11,000

Answer [ ]

102 A computer depreciates by 20 per cent of its original value each year. If it cost new £2,400, what is its value after three years?

A	B	C	D	E
£840	£960	£1,230	£1,360	£1,540

Answer [ ]

103 If it rains on 73 days a year in Italy, what are the odds that it will rain on any given day?

A	B	C	D	E
4 to 1	5 to 1	6 to 1	10 to 1	20 to 1

Answer [ ]

104 Tossing two coins, what is the probability that at least one is a head?

A	B	C
1/2	2/3	3/4

Answer [ ]

105 Tossing two coins, what is the probability that both coins are heads?

A	B	C
1/4	1/2	3/4

Answer

106 If tossing three coins, what is the possibility that at least one is a head?

A	B	C
5/8	6/8	7/8

Answer

107 If tossing three coins, what is the probability that none of them are heads?

A	B	C
1/2	1/4	1/8

Answer

Using the equations below, answer the following questions.

$$Y_1 = X^2 + 1$$
$$Y_2 = 2$$

108 For what X values are $Y_1 = Y_2$?

A	B	C	D
$X = 0$	$X = 2$	$X = 3$	$X = 1$

Answer

109 The following is true: $Y_1 > Y_2$

A	B	C
for all	for all	for all
$X > 0$	$X < -1$	$X < 0.5$

Answer

Chapter 4
Data interpretation

This type of test comprises tables, graphs or charts of information which you must interpret in order to answer the questions.

Be careful to rely only on the information that is given, even if you believe it to be wrong or out of date. It often pays to examine the questions before spending too much time interpreting the data.

Practise on the following questions. Answers are given in Part Three.

TEAM	Won	Drawn	Lost	Points
A	3	1	0	10
B	3	0	1	9
C	2	0	2	6
D	2	0	2	6
E	0	1	2	1
F	0	0	3	0

The above table shows the results and points scored from a league of six teams. Using this table answer the following questions:

1   How many points are given for:

  A   B   C
a win? a draw? a loss?

Answer [ ]

2   How many games have been played?

  A   B   C   D   E
  8   9   10   11   12

Answer [ ]

3   If each team plays every other team once during the season, how many games remain to be played?

  A   B   C   D   E
  4   5   6   7   8

Answer [ ]

4   The team with the most points at the end of the season wins the league. How many teams could achieve this?

  A   B   C   D   E
  1   2   3   4   5

Answer [ ]

5   The team with the least points at the end of the season wins the league. How many teams can finish bottom of the table?

  A   B   C   D   E
  1   2   3   4   5

Answer [ ]

6   What is the highest possible value for the points of all the teams combined at the end of the season?

  A   B   C   D   E
  40   41   42   43   44

Answer [ ]

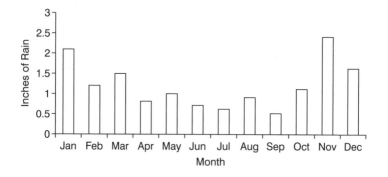

The above graph shows rainfall for a given country in terms of inches of rainfall per month. Using this graph answer the following questions:

7

    a. Which month had the highest level of rainfall?

    b. Which month had the lowest level of rainfall?

Answer ⬚

8 Which month had the highest absolute increase in rainfall compared to the previous month?

A	B	C	D	E
November	December	January	February	March

Answer ⬚

9 Which month had the highest decrease in rainfall compared to the previous month?

A	B	C	D	E
November	December	January	February	March

Answer ⬚

10 Which month had the lowest increase in rainfall compared to the previous month?

A	B	C	D	E
February	March	April	May	June

Answer ⬚

11   What is the total rainfall for the year?

A	B	C	D	E
4.4	14.4	24.4	34.4	44.4

Answer [   ]

12   Which month was closest to the average monthly rainfall for the year?

A	B	C	D	E
February	March	April	May	June

Answer [   ]

The following graph shows the average breakdown of monthly expenses for a household. Using this graph as a starting point, answer the following questions:

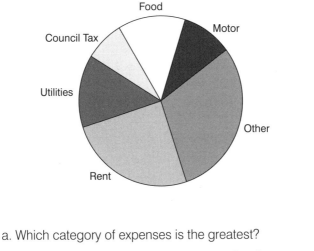

13

a. Which category of expenses is the greatest?

b. Which category of expenses is the smallest?

Answer [   ]

14 Which of the following best estimates the percentage of expenditure that goes towards rent?

A	B	C	D	E
10%	18%	25%	31%	48%

Answer [   ]

15 If the average total expenditure each month is £1,440 per month, how much is spent on rent?

A	B	C	D	E
£300	£310	£320	£340	£360

Answer [   ]

16 If a flat rate of 25 per cent is payable on all income, how much must be earned to pay for the rent alone?

A	B	C	D	E
£450	£460	£470	£480	£490

Answer [   ]

17 If the rent costs £360 per month, the household saves 20 per cent of its income after tax each month and tax is paid at a flat rate of 25 per cent on all income, how much does the household earn before tax each year?

A	B	C	D	E
£28,000	£28,400	£28,600	£28,800	£29,000

Answer [   ]

18 In the scenario in question 17, how much does the household save per year?

A	B	C	D	E
£2,420	£2,620	£2,820	£4,020	£4,320

Answer [   ]

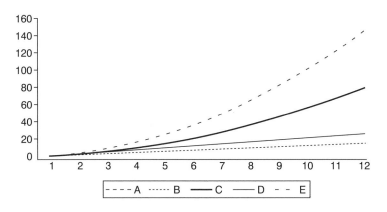

The above graph shows the population levels of five bacteria cultures measured every hour over a period of 12 hours. Using this graph answer the following questions (please note: line A runs along the *x* axis):

19 The rate of growth of culture A is best described as:

A B C
Zero Linear Exponential

Answer [   ]

20 The rate of growth of culture B is best described as:

A B C
Zero Linear Exponential

Answer [   ]

21 The rate of growth of culture C is best described as:

A B C
Zero Linear Exponential

Answer [   ]

22 The rate of growth of culture D is best described as:

A B C
Zero Linear Exponential

Answer [   ]

23 The rate of growth of culture E is best described as:

A   B   C
Zero   Linear   Exponential

Answer [   ]

Still referring to the last graph, and considering the following equations where P represents population and h represents hours elapsed, answer the following questions:

Equation i) $P = 2h$

Equation ii) $P = h$

Equation iii) $P = h^2$

Equation iv) $P = h \times 2$

Equation v) $P = h^2 - h$

Equation vi) $P[i] = P[i - 1] + h$,
                    where $P[i]$ is the population at hour i

Equation vii) $P = 0$

Equation viii) $P = 1$

Equation ix) $P = P$

Equation x) $P = h^3$

24 Which of the above equations best describes the apparent growth of culture A?

Answer [   ]

25 Which of the above equations best describes the apparent growth of culture B?

Answer [   ]

26 Which of the above equations best describes the apparent growth of culture C?

Answer [   ]

27   Which of the above equations best describes the apparent growth of culture D?

Answer [   ]

28   Which of the above equations best describes the apparent growth of culture E?

Answer [   ]

29   On the basis of the information given, what would be the best estimate of the bacterial population of culture A after 16 hours?

A	B	C	D	E
1	2	3	4	5

Answer [   ]

30   On the basis of the information given, what would be the best estimate of the bacterial population of culture D after 200 hours?

A	B	C	D	E
200	300	400	500	600

Answer [   ]

Examine the graphs below and answer the questions that follow:

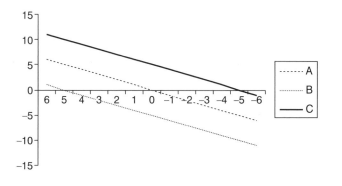

31   Which of A, B or C fits the formula
$y = x - 5$?

Answer [   ]

32   At which point does line C cross the x axis?

A	B	C	D	E
−1	−2	−3	−4	−5

Answer _____

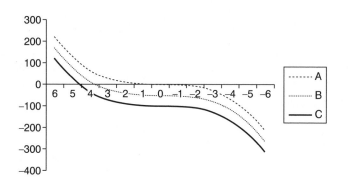

33   Which of A, B or C fits the formula $y = x^3$?

Answer _____

34   At which point does the line A cross the x axis?

A	B	C	D	E
0	1	2	3	4

Answer _____

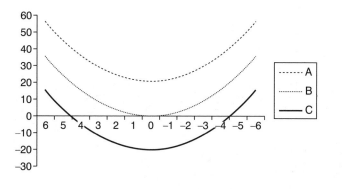

35   Which of A, B or C fits the formula
$y = x^2 + 20$?   *Answer* _____

36   At which approximate points does line C cross the x axis?

A	B	C	D	E
0	2 and 2	2 and –2	4.4 and 4.5	4.5 and –4.5

Answer [ ]

From the graph below, match the lines to the equations.

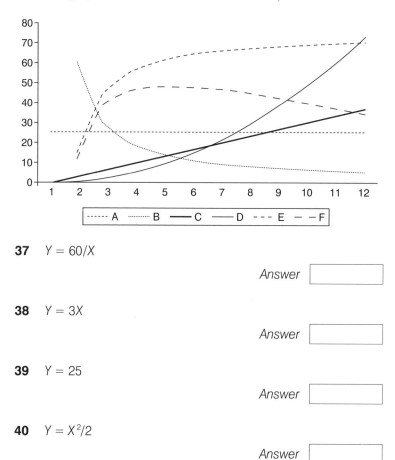

37 $Y = 60/X$

Answer [ ]

38 $Y = 3X$

Answer [ ]

39 $Y = 25$

Answer [ ]

40 $Y = X^2/2$

Answer [ ]

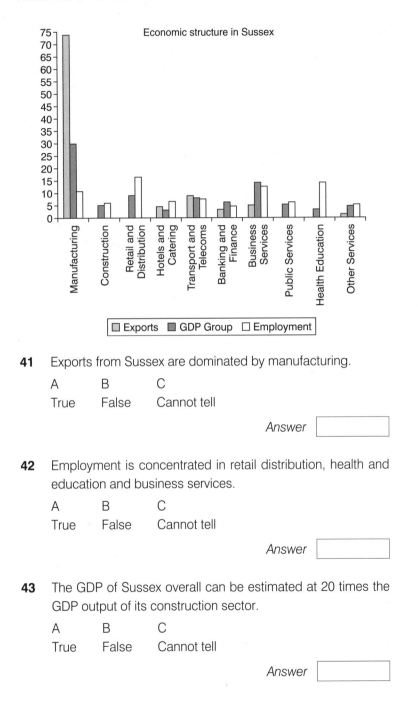

41   Exports from Sussex are dominated by manufacturing.

   A   B   C
   True   False   Cannot tell

                              Answer [   ]

42   Employment is concentrated in retail distribution, health and education and business services.

   A   B   C
   True   False   Cannot tell

                              Answer [   ]

43   The GDP of Sussex overall can be estimated at 20 times the GDP output of its construction sector.

   A   B   C
   True   False   Cannot tell

                              Answer [   ]

44 Assuming all values are integers, there are five prime numbers in the GDP output of manufacturing.

A   B   C
True   False   Cannot tell

Answer

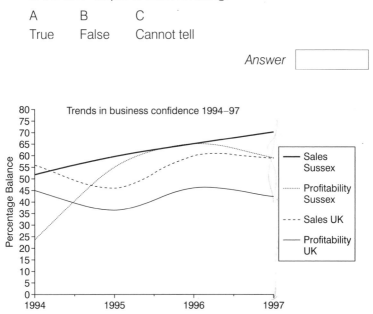

Trends in business confidence 1994-97

Sales
Sussex

Profitability
Sussex

Sales UK

Profitability
UK

Using the above graph, answer the following questions:

45 The graph demonstrates that the Sussex economy has grown faster than the UK economy overall.

A   B   C
True   False   Cannot tell

Answer

46 In 1997 the balance of businesses increased sales over previous years.

A   B   C
True   False   Cannot tell

Answer

47   In 1996 the balance of Sussex businesses reporting an increase in sales over those reporting decreasing sales was 65 per cent.

A   B   C
True   False   Cannot tell

Answer [   ]

48   Confidence in sales and profitability in Sussex during the period illustrated is more positive than in the UK as a whole.

A   B   C
True   False   Cannot tell

Answer [   ]

Amount of information

	% saying *About Right*	*Too Much*	*Not Enough*
Choice of course	65	1	28
Choice of training co.	59	0	33
Induction at college	64	2	14
Induction at placement	83	2	9
NVQ quals	68	1	18
How training taught	73	0	12
Job prospects	60	0	36
Expected	50		
Target	75		

A survey was conducted to deduce whether students felt they had received enough information regarding their training courses. From the results above answer the following questions:

49   The survey findings were overall short of the target of 75 per cent of respondents saying about the right amount of information.

A   B   C
True   False   Cannot tell

Answer [   ]

50 From the information given you can deduce that a total of only six respondents reported instances when too much information was provided.

A   B   C
True   False   Cannot tell

Answer [   ]

Vehicle	Speed
Bicycle	20 miles/h
Car	100 miles/h
Sports car	150 miles/h
Scooter	30 miles/h

Above are the speeds of four different vehicles. Using this table answer the following questions:

51 How far has the car travelled after 20 minutes?

A   B   C
20 miles   33.3 miles   40 miles

Answer [   ]

52 How long will it take the scooter to travel 40 miles?

A   B   C
1h 5 min   1h 20 min   1h 15 min

Answer [   ]

53 If the car and the sports car start at the same time, how much further has the sports car travelled after 30 minutes?

A   B   C
20 miles   28 miles   25 miles

Answer [   ]

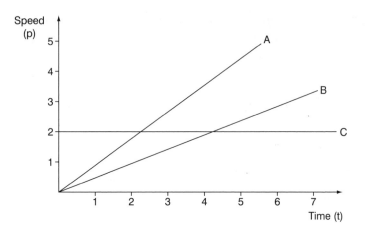

Above is a graph of three vehicles A, B and C, showing their speed *p* at time *t*. Using this graph, answer the following questions:

54 Which vehicle is moving fastest at time 4?

A   B   C

Answer ☐

55 Which vehicle is moving the fastest at time 1?

A   B   C

Answer ☐

56 Which vehicle has the slowest rate of acceleration?

A   B   C

Answer ☐

57 At what time are vehicles B and C travelling at the same speed?

1   2   4

Answer ☐

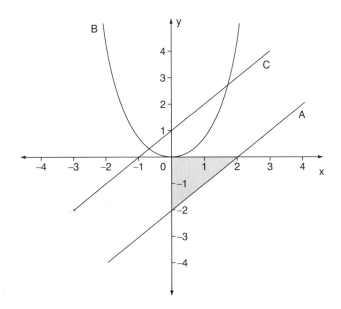

Use the graph above to answer the following questions:

58 Which equation describes C best?

A	B	C
$Y = X - 2$	$Y = X + 1$	$Y = X^2$

Answer [   ]

59 For function B, what is the value of Y when $X = -1/4$?

A	B	C
0.0750	0.0625	1.250

Answer [   ]

60 What is the area of the shadowed region in the graph?

A	B	C
3	4	2

Answer [   ]

61   Which equation describes B best?

A	B	C
$Y = X + 4$	$Y = 1 + X^2$	$Y = X^2$

Answer [   ]

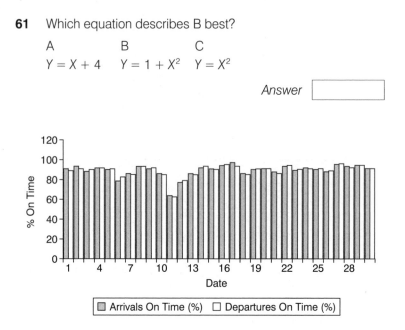

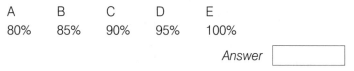

The chart above illustrates the percentage of flights arriving and departing on time from an airport during September. Use this chart to answer the following questions:

62   Over the month the average number of flights arriving or departing on time is approximately:

A	B	C	D	E
80%	85%	90%	95%	100%

Answer [   ]

63   The percentage of flights arriving on time is approximately proportional to the percentage of flights departing on time:

A	B	C
True	False	Cannot tell

Answer [   ]

64 On which date do the highest percentage of flights arrive on time?

A	B	C	D	E
15th	16th	17th	18th	19th

Answer ☐

65 On which date do the highest percentage of flights depart on time?

A	B	C	D	E
23rd	24th	25th	26th	27th

Answer ☐

66 Fog closes the airport for two hours one morning. Which date is this most likely to have happened on?

A	B	C	D	E
10th	11th	12th	13th	14th

Answer ☐

67 Is the airport more efficient during:

A The first four days of the month?

B The last four days of the month?

Answer ☐

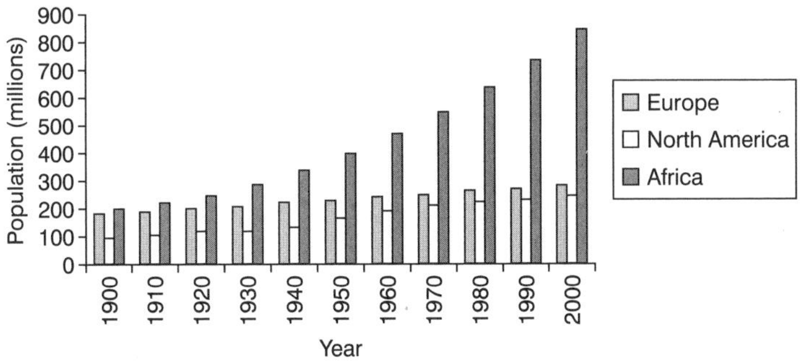

The chart above shows the populations of Europe, North America and Africa at 10-year intervals between 1900 and 2000. Use this chart to answer the following questions:

68   Which continent experiences:

a. The highest percentage growth during the century?

b. The lowest percentage growth during the century?

Answer [   ]

69   How many decades does it take for the population of North America to double from 1900?

Answer [   ]

70   How many decades does it take for the population of Africa to treble from 1900?

Answer [   ]

71   During the 1960s does the rate of growth in the North American population increase or decrease?

Answer [   ]

72   Which continent has the most consistent level of population throughout the century?

Answer [   ]

73   Is the rate of growth of population in North America higher during:

A   The first two decades of the century?

B   The last two decades of the century?

Answer [   ]

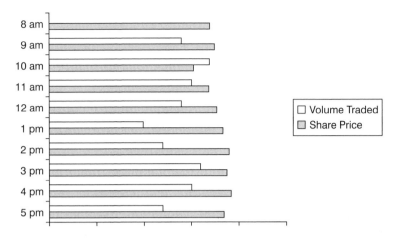

The above chart shows the price of a share and the number of shares traded in the previous hour. Use this graph to answer the questions below:

74 During which hour were:
   a. the most shares traded?
   b. the fewest shares traded?

   Answer [   ]

75 Overall, did the share lose or gain value during the day?   *Answer* [   ]

76 During which hour did the share lose the most value?   *Answer* [   ]

77 Which hour saw the greatest drop in the level of share trades?   *Answer* [   ]

78 Which saw the highest levels of trading – the first four hours of the day or the last four hours of the day?

   Answer [   ]

79 If a trader could only buy and sell once during the day, what would the best time have been to buy and sell?

Answer [   ]

Figures (a) and (b) below show people's primary sources of news information in 1995 and 2000. Using these charts, answer the following questions:

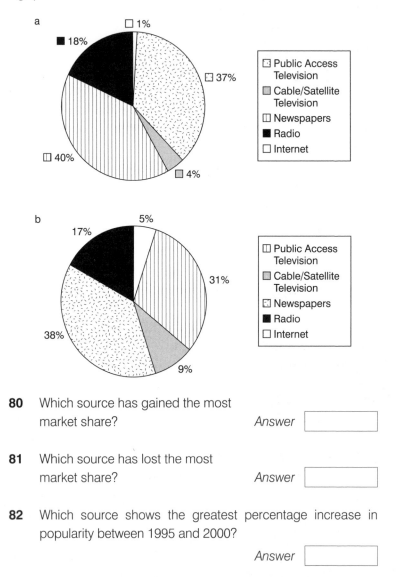

80 Which source has gained the most market share?

Answer [   ]

81 Which source has lost the most market share?

Answer [   ]

82 Which source shows the greatest percentage increase in popularity between 1995 and 2000?

Answer [   ]

83 Which source shows the smallest relative decrease in popularity during the period?

Answer [   ]

84 What is the overall percentage decrease in terms of all television (Public Access and Cable)?

A	B	C	D	E
1.0%	1.5%	2.0%	2.5%	3.0%

Answer [   ]

85 If the market continues to change in this way, what would the internet share of the market be likely to be in 2005?

A	B	C	D	E
10%	15%	20%	25%	30%

Answer [   ]

From the graph above, answer the following questions:

86 a. In what month were oil prices lowest?

A	B	C	D	E
January	February	March	April	May

Answer [ ]

b. In what month were petrol prices highest?

A	B	C	D	E
July	August	September	October	November

Answer [ ]

87 Which month saw the highest increase in crude oil prices?

A	B	C	D	E
March	April	May	June	July

Answer [ ]

88 Which two consecutive months saw the highest increase in petrol prices?

A	B	C	D	E
February & March	April & May	June & July	August & September	October & November

Answer [ ]

89 Which month sees the highest increase in petrol prices compared relative to oil prices?

A	B	C	D	E
May	June	July	August	September

Answer [ ]

90 Estimate the highest price that crude oil prices reach during the year.

A	B	C	D	E
2.0	2.1	2.2	2.3	2.4

Answer [ ]

91   What is the price of petrol in April?

A	B	C	D	E
3.0	3.1	3.2	3.3	3.4

Answer [   ]

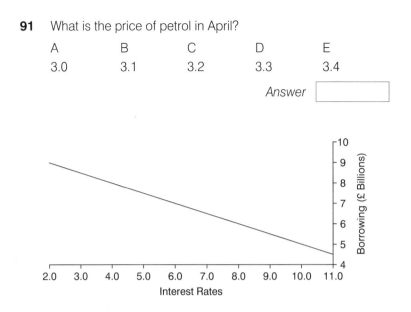

Interest Rates

The above graph shows an example of the relationship between interest rates and monthly borrowing by the public. From this graph answer the following:

92   If interest rates are set at 6 per cent, how much will people borrow in a month?

A	B	C	D	E
£6 billion	£7 billion	£8 billion	£9 billion	£10 billion

Answer [   ]

93   If the Bank of England cuts interest rates by 2 per cent, by how much will monthly borrowing increase?

A	B	C	D	E
No change in rate	£1 billion	£2 billion	£3 billion	£225 million

Answer [   ]

94 How much would the Bank of England need to increase interest rates by to reduce borrowing by £2 billion per month?

A	B	C	D	E
3%	4%	5%	6%	7%

Answer [   ]

95 If interest rates average 7.5 per cent during a year, how much borrowing will take place during the year?

A	B	C	D	E
£55 billion	£65 billion	£75 billion	£85 billion	£95 billion

Answer [   ]

96 If interest rates are 6.25 per cent from 1 January to 31 March, 6.5 per cent from 1 April to 30 September and 6.75 per cent for the rest of the year, how much borrowing will take place during the year?

A	B	C	D	E
£78 billion	£79 billion	£80 billion	£81 billion	£82 billion

Answer [   ]

97 In this example borrowing is:

A   directly proportional

B   inversely proportional to interest rates.

Answer [   ]

Chapter 5
Business judgement

Real business judgement-type tests seek to assess the core competencies required by commerce. They make use of the context of business and draw examples from it. The language used is drawn from the workplace. The questions should not require highly specialized knowledge but may examine the extent to which you can use the basic vocabulary and principal operations of business. These are the kind of thing that any interested person would acquire from reading, for example, the quality press. You do not need any particular work experience in order to answer the questions.

The questions in this chapter allow practice in business comprehension, basic finance and business judgement.

Business comprehension

1 Which of the following is an example of stocks?

A	B	C	D
Bonds	Options	Futures	Shares

Answer [　　　　]

2 Which of the following is an example of income?

A	B	C	D
Expenditure	Credit	Debit	Revenue

Answer [　　　　]

3 Which of the following is an example of bonds?

A	B	C	D
Fixed-income securities	Equity	Mutual funds	Stocks

Answer [　　　　]

4 Which of the following is an example of yield?

A	B	C	D
Interest	Earnings	Capital	Investment

Answer [　　　　]

5 Which of the following is an example of acquisition?

A	B	C	D
Merger	Joint venture	Purchase	Redundancy

Answer [　　　　]

6 Which of the following is an example of capital?

A	B	C	D
Input	Output	Loan	Resources

Answer [　　　　]

7 Which of the following is an example of equilibrium?

A	B	C	D
Supply	Demand	Change	Balance

Answer [   ]

8 Which of the following is an example of inflation?

A   Decrease of demand

B   Increase of demand

C   Decrease in price levels

D   Increase in price levels

Answer [   ]

9 Which of the following is an example of oligopoly?

A   Many firms in the market

B   One firm in the market

C   A few firms in the market

D   Many firms in the market but
with differentiated products

Answer [   ]

10 Which of the following is an example of Human Resources?

A	B	C	D
Staff	Employer	Clients	Student

Answer [   ]

Basic finance

	Q1 (£'000)	Q2 (£'000)	Q3 (£'000)	Q4 (£'000)
Sales	500	550	525	600
Misc. income	50	100	50	75
Cost of goods sold	100	100	75	125
Gross profit	450	550	500	550

11 Calculate the miscellaneous income for quarters 1 and 4.

A	B	C	D
£100	£75,000	£175	£125,000

Answer [   ]

12 What is the total sale figure for all four quarters?

A	B	C	D
£2,175	£2,250	£2,175,000	£2,250,000

Answer [   ]

13 How great is the miscellaneous income as a ratio of the total income for the whole year?

A	B	C	D
11%	0.011	11	100%

Answer [   ]

Passage 1

Only market forces can solve the problem of high broadband prices in the UK, says Oftel director general David Edmonds. At £25 to £35 per month, UK prices are higher than the United States, France, Germany and Sweden.

14 How much does a high broadband user have to pay per year in the UK?

A	B	C	D
£25 to £35	£300 to £420	£275 to £400	£250 to £350

Answer [   ]

15 If users in the United States were to pay £20 per month, what percentage of the cost to UK users would that represent?

A	B	C	D
60–80%	10–15%	2–5%	120–140%

Answer [   ]

Passage 2

At present, BT's free voicemail service is growing at a rate of 20,000 users a day – with each user of the service able to store up to 20 minutes of incoming messages at any one time.

16 How many users does the BT service attract per year?

A	B	C	D
730,000	7,300	7,300,000	73,000

Answer [ ]

17 How many hours of incoming messages can the new users store at any one time?

A	B	C	D
6,666 h	400,000 h	40,000 h	66,666 h

Answer [ ]

Passage 3

Bank of Granite's average loan margin – the difference between the interest it pays depositors and the interest it collects from borrowers – is 5 per cent, a full percentage point over the industry mean.

18 What is the average loan margin of other banks?

A	B	C	D
1.5%	0.5%	4%	0.4%

Answer [ ]

Passage 4

British Airways remains one of the world's most successful airlines. In 1996–97, it announced pre-tax profits up by 10 per cent on the previous year to £650 million.

19 Calculate the pre-tax profit for 1995–96.

A	B	C	D
£590 million	£670 million	£520 million	£500 million

Answer [ ]

20   Given a tax rate of 25 per cent, calculate the net profit for 1996–97.

A	B	C	D
£812.5 million	£487.5 million	£715 million	£675.5 million

Answer [   ]

	Tons produced/ year	Tons sold/ year	Tons exported/ year
Factory A	5.5	4	0
Factory B	64	60	50
Factory C	40	40	40
Factory D	80	50	10

21   How many tons do the four factories not sell?

A	B	C	D
20	35.5	36.5	38.5

Answer [   ]

22   Which factory has the highest export ratio?

A, B, C or D?

Answer [   ]

23   Which factory has the lowest sales ratio?

A, B, C or D?

Answer [   ]

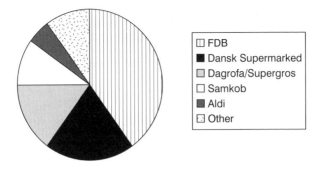

The above chart shows the breakdown of the main retail grocery stores in Denmark. Using this chart as a starting point, answer the following questions:

24   Which retail store has the largest share of the market?   *Answer* [＿＿＿＿＿]

25   What two groups of retail stores have exactly the same presence on the Danish market?

Answer [＿＿＿＿＿]

26   How large is the share of the second largest retail store?

A	B	C	D
10%	1/5	0.75	30%

Answer [＿＿＿＿＿]

27   How large is the share of the three smallest groups together?

A	B	C	D
1/4	33%	0.75	20%

Answer [＿＿＿＿＿]

28   There are 3,500 retail outlets in Denmark. How many of these are FDB outlets?

A	B	C	D
500	1,000	2,000	1,400

Answer [＿＿＿＿＿]

29 How many retail stores do the three largest groups have together?

A	B	C	D
875	2,625	2,000	3,000

Answer [ ]

Business comprehension

Unisys wins $40 million BT voicemail deal.

30 BT will pay Unisys $40 million for its services.

A	B	C
True	False	Cannot tell

Answer [ ]

31 Unisys will make large profits by selling its services to BT.

A	B	C
True	False	Cannot tell

Answer [ ]

Tyco shares closed down $8.35 at $33.65 – their lowest level for more than two years – despite assurances from the company that investors' fears were unfounded.

32 Shares haven't been this low for more than three years.

A	B	C
True	False	Cannot tell

Answer [ ]

33 The closing price that day was $8.35.

A	B	C
True	False	Cannot tell

Answer [ ]

34   The company told shareholders not to worry.

A   B   C
True   False   Cannot tell

Answer [   ]

Haji-Ioannou, owner of easyJet, explained that its strategy is 'based on the belief that demand for short-haul air transport is price elastic'.

35   easyJet is a low-fares airline.

A   B   C
True   False   Cannot tell

Answer [   ]

36   Haji-Ioannou believes that the lower the price of a plane ticket, the higher is the demand.

A   B   C
True   False   Cannot tell

Answer [   ]

37   Haji-Ioannou believes that the higher the price of a plane ticket, the lower is the demand.

A   B   C
True   False   Cannot tell

Answer [   ]

The primary driver of the boom in commodity export markets has been the weak Australian dollar. It has fallen from US$0.80 over the past five years to around US$0.51 today.

38   Major parts of Australian exports are commodities.

A   B   C
True   False   Cannot tell

Answer [   ]

39 The US dollar has strengthened its value against the Australian dollar over the past five years.

A   B   C
True   False   Cannot tell

Answer [＿＿＿＿＿]

40 The US dollar is stronger against the Australian dollar today than it was three years ago.

A   B   C
True   False   Cannot tell

Answer [＿＿＿＿＿]

Belgium is one of the world's leading exporters of beer. In 1994 it exported over 31 per cent of its production, almost all to other EU countries.

41 Belgium exported 69 per cent of its beer produced in 1994 to non-EU countries.

A   B   C
True   False   Cannot tell

Answer [＿＿＿＿＿]

42 Belgian beer is the most exported beer in the world.

A   B   C
True   False   Cannot tell

Answer [＿＿＿＿＿]

43 31 per cent of Belgian exports go to other EU countries.

A   B   C
True   False   Cannot tell

Answer [＿＿＿＿＿]

44 31 per cent of Belgian production in 1994 was beer.

A   B   C
True   False   Cannot tell

Answer ⬚

Business judgement

Suppose that as a part of the EU's Common Agriculture Policy it was decided that egg producers were guaranteed a minimum price for eggs and that any surplus of eggs would be bought up by the government at the agreed price.

Using the graph below, answer the following questions:

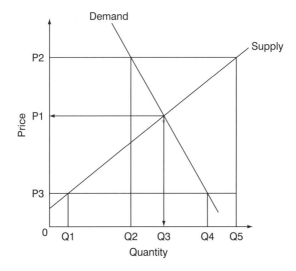

45 What would be the equilibrium price and quantity in the absence of any intervention?

Answer ⬚

46 If the government were to guarantee a price of P2, how many eggs would the government have to buy up?

A   B   C   D   E
Q1 demand   Q2 supply   Q3 supply   Q4–Q2   Q5–Q2

Answer ⬚

47 What would be the quantity of eggs demanded by households at this price?

A   B   C   D   E
Q1   Q2   Q3   Q4   Q5

Answer [   ]

48 What would be the market price if the government were to agree a minimum price of P3?

A   B   C
P1   P2   P3

Answer [   ]

49 What would be the demand from households at this price?

A   B   C   D   E
Q1   Q2   Q3   Q4   Q5

Answer [   ]

The following diagram shows the cost curves of a firm under perfect competition. Use it to answer the following questions.

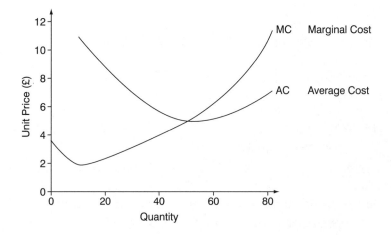

50 How much will the firm produce in order to maximize profits at a price of £8/unit?

A	B	C	D
50 units	60 units	70 units	80 units

Answer [   ]

51 What will the firm's average cost of production be at this output?

A	B	C
£6 per unit	£8 per unit	£10 per unit

Answer [   ]

52 How much profit will the firm make at this cost and output?

A	B	C
£70	£140	£2

Answer [   ]

53 At the price of £4/unit, how many units will be produced, and will any profit be generated?

A	B	C	D
40 units with profit	40 units, no profit	20 units with profit	20 units, no profit

Answer [   ]

Market research findings relating to 'Royal Tea'

Market A	Market B
Competitor brands are winning Royal Tea's market share	Market leading brand
Price sensitive market	Sold at a premium price
Customers base buy decision almost entirely on price	High level of customer loyalty (low level of brand switching)
Brand is sold at modest premium over competitors	Customers perceive higher price to imply higher quality

Value of total sales of Royal Tea (000s)

Market A	$120	$121	$115	$119
Market B	$20	$19	$18	$19
	2002	2004	2006	2008

Use the information provided to answer the following questions:

54 Which of the following measures would most likely help improve sales in market A?

A improved branding

B increased advertising

C discount coupons

D more sales representatives

Answer [ ]

55 Which set of information would you include in an estimation of fixed costs at Royal Tea?

A utility and raw material costs

B staff and building rent

C building maintenance and taxes

D sales commissions and returns

Answer [ ]

56 Which of the two markets would you judge to be best suited to niche marketing techniques?

A   B

Answer [ ]

57 Which of the following statements if true would best support the assumption that most of Royal Tea customers were women?

A Women traditionally do the shopping.

B The sales trend over the last few years mirrors the population trend towards a larger proportion of women in the overall population.

C In an awareness survey women were found to be three times more aware of the Royal Tea brand than men.

D Stores that sell into Market B are predominately located in urban areas that comprise a disproportionate number of women.

Answer

---

58 Which measure would NOT help sales in market B?

A Lower the price

B Increase marketing

C Increase the price by a small percentage

D Cannot tell

Answer

---

59 Which conclusion in the findings of the market research seem not to be supported by the sales figures?

A Market leading brand – market B

B Brand is sold at modest premium over competitors – market A

C Competitor brands are winning Royal Tea's market share – market A

D High level of customer loyalty (low level of brand switching) – market B

Answer

---

60 Which of the following activities would best suit a push sales strategy for market A?

A Set up tasting stalls in stores that stock Royal Tea

B Monitor competitor prices and fix the price at a premium to those prices

C Offer lower prices at stores where sales are disappointing

D Recruit more sales representatives

Answer

Chapter 6
Data sufficiency

Tests of data sufficiency seek to measure a candidate's ability to evaluate information and identify logical connections. These types of question do not require you to provide the answer but to establish if the statement is true or false, or indicate whether or not the question can be answered, or identify from a list of options which further information you require in order to answer the question. The subject matter can be drawn from almost any subject.

Take care to rely only on the information given in order to answer the questions. Be especially careful if the questions relate to a subject on which you know a great deal, as you must resist the temptation to bring your own knowledge to the problem.

The following questions seek to provide practice ranging from easy to difficult in the main styles of this type of test.

Situation 1

Tim Chou, president of oracle.com, believes the company could take between 10 and 20 per cent of its European business online within the next 12 months, despite a slow start in Europe.

1   Oracle has been very successful in Europe.

A   B   C
True   False   Cannot tell

Answer [   ]

2   10–20 per cent of Oracle's business has been online for the past 12 months.

A   B   C
True   False   Cannot tell

Answer [   ]

Situation 2

One-bedroom flats were the most popular new homes in London last year, both for living and as investments. The good news is that more of these flats are being built; the bad news is that they are getting smaller and more expensive.

3   It has become popular to buy flats as investments in London.

A   B   C
True   False   Cannot tell

Answer [   ]

4   One-bedroom flats are becoming more expensive.

A   B   C
True   False   Cannot tell

Answer [   ]

5   Buyers who look to invest often rent out their flats.

A   B   C
True   False   Cannot tell

Answer [   ]

Situation 3

The number of IT jobs in the UK has more than doubled in the last five years. But while women represent over half of the potential workforce in the UK, they form only 22 per cent of the IT workforce, compared with 29 per cent as recently as 2004, according to government figures.

6 More than 50 per cent of the potential workforce in the UK are women.

A	B	C
True	False	Cannot tell

Answer [   ]

7 The IT workforce is dominated by women.

A	B	C
True	False	Cannot tell

Answer [   ]

8 7 per cent of women working in IT have moved to work elsewhere.

A	B	C
True	False	Cannot tell

Answer [   ]

9 There are fewer women working in IT today than in 1997.

A	B	C
True	False	Cannot tell

Answer [   ]

Situation 4

Seen over a longer period, however, Sweden's readiness to let people in has indeed lessened. Its generous laws resulted in about 80 per cent of claimants being allowed to stay during the 1970s and 1980s. From 1990 that figure dropped to 40 per cent, after the stricter asylum criteria that apply today were adopted. The tougher rules have not deterred new applicants: asylum claims rose by 45 per cent last year to 16,000. Swedish officials say that organized asylum traffic and human smuggling by racketeers has bumped up the figures.

10 Sweden has always had a very harsh asylum policy.

A   B   C
True   False   Cannot tell

Answer [   ]

11 Only 20 per cent of claiming asylum seekers were turned away during the 1970s and 1980s.

A   B   C
True   False   Cannot tell

Answer [   ]

12 There are fewer asylum seekers this year than there were last year.

A   B   C
True   False   Cannot tell

Answer [   ]

13 Last year the number of asylum seekers rose by almost a half.

A   B   C
True   False   Cannot tell

Answer [   ]

14 Organized asylum traffic and human smuggling is on the increase.

A   B   C
True   False   Cannot tell

Answer [   ]

15 There were approximately 8,000 asylum claims made two years ago.

A   B   C
True   False   Cannot tell

Answer [   ]

Situation 5

Britain's countryside has not yet returned to normal. More than 80 per cent of the country's footpaths remain closed. But at least farmers are beginning to see the end of their nightmare. The cost of the outbreak has been high. Last week, the Centre for Economic and Business Research estimated that the epidemic would cost farmers £3.6 billion ($5.2 billion). The government estimates that tourism is still losing £125 million a week, and the British Tourist Authority (BTA) says that on current trends Britain could lose up to £2.5 billion over the year in revenue from overseas tourists.

16 More than 80 per cent of Britain's farms remain closed.

A   B   C
True   False   Cannot tell

Answer [   ]

17 British farmers have lost just over $3.6 billion because of foot-and-mouth disease.

A   B   C
True   False   Cannot tell

Answer [   ]

18 The BTA believes that the number of tourists from abroad will decrease.

A   B   C
True   False   Cannot tell

Answer [   ]

19 Britain is losing out on overseas tourists because of the epidemic.

A   B   C
True   False   Cannot tell

Answer [   ]

20 The Centre for Economic and Business Research estimates that the tourism industry is still losing £125 million a week.

A   B   C
True   False   Cannot tell

Answer [   ]

The following 33 data sufficiency questions do not relate to a situation or passage.

21 A 6 lb baby whose weight doubles every day will weigh more than eighteen 40-stone elephants in under two weeks.
(NB 1 stone = 14 lb)

A   B   C
True   False   Cannot tell

Answer [   ]

22 The white triangle has three-fifths the area of the shaded section.

A   B   C
True   False   Cannot tell

Answer [   ]

23 In a triathlon, an athlete swims for 20 minutes at 10 mph, cycles for 30 minutes at 20 mph and runs for 10 minutes at 10 mph. The total distance covered is 12 miles.

A   B   C
True   False   Cannot tell

Answer

24 A yacht sails for one hour at an average speed of 10 mph. If the yacht makes one tack of 90 degrees, the straight-line distance between the starting and finishing points is 7.07 N miles.

A   B   C
True   False   Cannot tell

Answer

25 If a heart beats once a second, it beats 30,536 times in a year.

A   B   C
True   False   Cannot tell

Answer

26 A car with a full 50-litre tank of petrol sets off on a journey of 740 miles. After travelling for four hours at 68 mph the driver slows down to conserve fuel – but will still run out of petrol more than 100 miles before reaching his destination.

A   B   C
True   False   Cannot tell

Answer

27 Typing at 25 words per minute, I can write up a 6,000-word report in less than an hour.

A   B   C
True   False   Cannot tell

Answer

28 A £15 bet placed at odds of 25:3 will yield a total of £125 if successful.

A	B	C
True	False	Cannot tell

Answer

29 The sum of the internal angles of an isosceles triangle will be exactly half of the sum of the internal angles of a square.

A	B	C
True	False	Cannot tell

Answer

30 A gym subscription is either £500 per year, or £50 per month over 12 months. It would be cheaper to borrow £500 from a bank for 12 months at an APR of 20 per cent and pay the gym in full rather than to pay monthly.

A	B	C
True	False	Cannot tell

Answer

31 A car constantly accelerating at 60 miles per hour from stand-still will have travelled 60 miles in one hour.

A	B	C
True	False	Cannot tell

Answer

32 A car constantly accelerating at 60 miles per hour from stand-still will have travelled 120 miles in two hours.

A	B	C
True	False	Cannot tell

Answer

33 If inflation is running at 10 per cent, a savings account yielding 9 per cent will lose value whilst money borrowed at a percentage rate of 9 per cent will gain value.

A   B   C
True   False   Cannot tell

Answer [   ]

34 A business with costs of £80,000 per month, which makes 16 per cent net profit on the products it markets, will need to generate sales of £500,000 per month to break even.

A   B   C
True   False   Cannot tell

Answer [   ]

35 25 people put a total of £75,000 into a savings fund with a variable interest rate fixed at 2.5 per cent above the Bank of England base rate which is 3.5 per cent when the fund is set up. When the fund is closed five years later, each of the investors will receive over £4,000.

A   B   C
True   False   Cannot tell

Answer [   ]

36 The area of an equilateral triangle with sides of 50 cm is half of the area of a square with sides of 50 cm.

A   B   C
True   False   Cannot tell

Answer [   ]

37 The combined area of the shaded triangles is x^2.

A   B   C
True   False   Cannot tell

Answer [   ]

38 In statistics, an example of discrete variable data would be the number of fish caught by a heron from a garden pond each year.

A   B   C
True   False   Cannot tell

Answer [   ]

39 An example of continuous variable data is the volume of water held in the garden pond measured each day over a hot summer.

A   B   C
True   False   Cannot tell

Answer [   ]

40 The symbol Σx represents the mean of x.

A   B   C
True   False   Cannot tell

Answer [   ]

41 $\bar{X}$ = The sample mean of X.

A   B   C
True   False   Cannot tell

Answer [   ]

42 Which of the following is the definition of average (a bit of a trick question?)

A The sample arithmetic mean

B The middle value with the sample ranked in increasing magnitude

C The value with the highest frequency

D None of these

Answer [   ]

43 Only proportional increases and not decreases are achieved using a multiplier.

A   B   C

True   False   Cannot tell

Answer [   ]

44 Quota sampling is used to draw representative conclusions that can be applied to the entire population.

A   B   C

True   False   Cannot tell

Answer [   ]

45 To change a percentage into a decimal, move the decimal point two places to the left. To change a percentage to a fraction, divide by 100.

A   B   C

True   False   Cannot tell

Answer [   ]

46 Events are mutually exclusive if the outcomes have no effect on each other. Independent events cannot happen at the same time.

A   B   C

True   False   Cannot tell

Answer [   ]

47 If a number can be divided into another it is a factor of that number. All numbers have factors.

A   B   C
True   False   Cannot tell

Answer [   ]

48 Multiplication and division are inverse operations. To multiply two fractions you can multiply the numerators and the denominators. By dividing the numerator by the denominator you can change a fraction into its decimal equivalent.

A   B   C
True   False   Cannot tell

Answer [   ]

49 In a bar chart the frequency of the data is shown by the area. In a histogram the frequency of the data is shown by the height. In a bar chart the frequency scale shows the actual frequency.

A   B   C
True   False   Cannot tell

Answer [   ]

50 The inter-quartile range is the difference between the lower quartile and upper quartile values. The upper quartile is two-thirds of the way through the data. The median is found halfway through the data.

A   B   C
True   False   Cannot tell

Answer [   ]

51 Cumulative frequency gives the running total. Correlation is a measurement of the strength of a relationship. The relative size of two or more quantities can be compared with a ratio.

A   B   C
True   False   Cannot tell

Answer [   ]

52 If data is symmetrical then the mean and median are equal. When a positive skew occurs the mean is less than the median. When a negative skew occurs the mean is more than the median.

A   B   C
True   False   Cannot tell

Answer [_____]

53 Probability measures uncertainty. Probability is measured on a scale of 0–1. Probability and possibility are interchangeable terms.

A   B   C
True   False   Cannot tell

Answer [_____]

Read the passage and use the information to answer the questions.

Passage 1

After expanding by 4 per cent last year, the world economy is expected to grow by just 1.5 per cent this year and by about the same rate next year. This would meet the definition of global recession – annual growth of less than 2 per cent. It would be the first time in ten years that the world economy has grown by less than 2 per cent for two consecutive years.

54 The three largest economies of the world, the United States, Japan and Germany, are either in recession or on the brink of it.

A   B   C
True   False   Cannot tell

Answer [_____]

55 The world economy is in recession.

A   B   C
True   False   Cannot tell

Answer [_____]

56 Global economic growth is on course to be its weakest for 10 years.

A   B   C
True   False   Cannot tell

Answer [   ]

Read the passage and use the information to answer the questions.

Passage 2

Recent data shows that the UK economy has slowed compared with a year ago. Annual growth averaged 2.3 per cent in the first three quarters this year against 2.9 per cent in those quarters during last year. This rate places the UK with the fastest growth rate of the G7 economies (the world's seven largest economies). This means that for the first time since the 1950s the UK has outperformed the other major economies during a recession. The Bank of England puts the chance of recession next year at 1 in 10.

57 In the past the UK has experienced a more severe recession than the other major world economies.

A   B   C
True   False   Cannot tell

Answer [   ]

58 The Bank of England defines recession as annual growth of less than 2 per cent and expects growth in the UK next year to be at 2 per cent or over.

A   B   C
True   False   Cannot tell

Answer [   ]

59 There is some evidence in the passage that supports the suggestion that the current global slowdown is having a negative impact on the UK economy.

A   B   C
True   False   Cannot tell

Answer [   ]

60 In contrast to the past 40 years, during a world recession the UK economy has continued to grow, although more slowly.

A   B   C
True   False   Cannot tell

Answer [   ]

Read the passage and answer the questions that follow.

Passage 3

Global low inflation and weak growth or recession are likely to lead to further cuts in interest rates. The projected economic cycles suggest that the United States will make a quicker recovery than Europe and that therefore the dollar will remain firm against the euro.

Continued debt and deflation in Japan is expected to keep the yen weak.

61 The euro is undervalued against the dollar.

A   B   C
True   False   Cannot tell

Answer [   ]

62 The interest rate-cutting cycle is not yet over.

A   B   C
True   False   Cannot tell

Answer [   ]

63 A reversal of recent monetary policy easing is forecast.

A   B   C
True   False   Cannot tell

Answer [   ]

Read the following passage and identify which of the statements are required in order to answer the questions that follow.

Passage 4

An employer pays all of his staff in terms of basic salary and bonus. In a very good month the bonus is greater than the basic salary for most of his staff. In a bad month the bonus can be zero.

- Sales staff receive the highest bonus payments but the lowest basic salaries.
- Production staff receive moderate bonus payments and moderate salaries.
- Administration staff receive the lowest bonus payments but the highest salaries.

Given the above information, which of the following statements are required to answer the questions below?

A Sales staff are the highest paid of all staff when sales exceed £1 million per month.

B Administration staff earn twice as much basic salary as sales staff.

C Production staff earn more than administration staff when sales exceed £1 million per month.

64 Administration staff stand to gain the least regardless of whether it is a good or bad month.

A Statement A

B Statement B

C Statement C

D Statements A and B

E Statements B and C

F Statements A and C

G Statements A, B and C

H None of the above

Answer ⬚

65 Administration staff earn less than all other staff if sales exceed £1 million.

A Statement A

B Statement B

C Statement C

D Statements A and B

E Statements B and C

F Statements A and C

G Statements A, B and C

H None of the above

Answer ⬚

66 If sales exceed £1 million in a month sales staff will receive a bonus which is greater than the basic salary of administration staff.

  A Statement A

  B Statement B

  C Statement C

  D Statements A and B

  E Statements B and C

  F Statements A and C

  G Statements A, B and C

  H None of the above

Answer [   ]

Passage 5

Fourteen people get on a bus at the start of its journey. There are three stops, including the final destination. In total the bus driver collects more than £4 and less than £6 in fares. All of the passengers have paid the correct fare for their intended journey. No one else gets on the bus before it reaches the final stop.

  A The cost of going to the first stop is 25p

  B The cost of going to the second stop is 45p

  C The cost of going to the last stop is 85p

  D None of the above

Which of the above statements are required in order to prove the following:

67 At least one passenger plans to leave the bus at the first stop.   *Answer* [   ]

68 Not all of the passengers plan to leave the bus at the first stop.   *Answer* [   ]

69   If there are eight passengers on the bus after the first stop, no more than six passengers can leave the bus at the second stop.

Answer [   ]

70   After the second stop at least 4 out of 11 passengers realize that they have missed their stops.

Answer [   ]

71   Read the passage and question below and decide if you need either both or neither statement in order to answer the question.

A family consisting of two adults and three children has booked a charter to Cyprus. The children are one, seven and ten years old. With children's discount, the whole trip costs £1,800. How much does the trip cost for the children?

1 The family pays £120 for the one-year-old.

2 The seven- and the ten-year-old each pay 40 per cent of the price of an adult.

There is sufficient information in order to solve the question:

A in (1) but not in (2)

B in (2) but not in (1)

C in (1) and (2) together

D in (1) and (2) separately

E in none of the statements

Answer [   ]

72   Read the question and decide if you need either both or neither statement in order to answer the question.

Jane has one red and one blue ball. What is the volume of the blue ball?

1 The volume of the red ball, which is smaller than the blue one, is 0.75 cm³. The balls are in the volume ratio of 2 to 3.

2 The radius of the blue ball is 50 per cent longer than the radius of the red ball.

There is sufficient information in order to solve the question:

A in (1) but not in (2)

B in (2) but not in (1)

C in (1) and (2) together

D in (1) and (2) separately

E in none of the statements

Answer [   ]

73   Read the question and decide if you need either both or neither statement in order to answer the question.

John writes down a number of whole numbers between 10 and 25. The number's mean value is 18. How many whole numbers has John written down?

1 The mean of the three first numbers that John writes down is 22.

2 The mean of the two last numbers that John writes down is 12.

There is sufficient information in order to solve the question:

A in (1) but not in (2)

B in (2) but not in (1)

C in (1) and (2) together

D in (1) and (2) separately

E in none of the statements

Answer [   ]

74 Read the question and decide if you need either both or neither statement in order to answer the question.

Sarah is taller than Mary. Anna is taller than Jenny. Who is the shortest?

1 Sarah is taller than Jenny.

2 Anna is shorter than Mary.

There is sufficient information in order to solve the question:

A in (1) but not in (2)

B in (2) but not in (1)

C in (1) and (2) together

D in (1) and (2) separately

E in none of the statements

Answer

75 Read the question and decide if you need either both or neither statement in order to answer the question.

Three hens lay x, y and z eggs respectively. How many eggs did they lay altogether?

1 $5y + x = 5z$

2 $z = 7$

There is sufficient information in order to solve the question:

A in (1) but not in (2)

B in (2) but not in (1)

C in (1) and (2) together

D in (1) and (2) separately

E in none of the statements

Answer

76 Read the question and decide if you need either both or neither statement in order to answer the question.

James, Barbara and Charles are together 90 years old. Charles is the same age as James and Barbara together. How old is Barbara?

1 James and Charles are together twice as old as Barbara.

2 In 15 years James will be half the age of Charles.

There is sufficient information in order to solve the question:

A in (1) but not in (2)

B in (2) but not in (1)

C in (1) and (2) together

D in (1) and (2) separately

E in none of the statements

Answer _____

77 Read the question and decide if you need either both or neither statement in order to answer the question.

Sarah walked home from the railway station. It took her longer to walk the first half of the distance than it took for her to walk the second half of the distance. How long did it take Sarah to walk the whole distance?

1 It took Sarah 30 minutes to walk the first half of the distance.

2 Sarah walked the second half at an average speed of 1 km/h faster than she had walked the first half.

There is sufficient information in order to solve the question:

A in (1) but not in (2)

B in (2) but not in (1)

C in (1) and (2) together

D in (1) and (2) separately

E in none of the statements

Answer [   ]

78 Read the question and decide if you need either both or neither statement in order to answer the question.

On a farm, there are 40 rabbits out of which 10 are white, 12 are black and 18 are speckled; 60 per cent of the rabbits are female. How many of the black rabbits are female?

1 10 of the black and the white rabbits are female.

2 14 of the speckled rabbits are female.

There is sufficient information in order to solve the question:

A in (1) but not in (2)

B in (2) but not in (1)

C in (1) and (2) together

D in (1) and (2) separately

E in none of the statements

Answer ☐

79   Read the question and decide if you need either both or neither statement in order to answer the question.

In a bowl there are marbles that are either blue, red or green; 75 marbles are red. How many marbles are there in the bowl?

1 50 per cent of the marbles in the bowl are either red or blue.

2 175 of the marbles in the bowl are either red or green.

There is sufficient information in order to solve the question:

A in (1) but not in (2)

B in (2) but not in (1)

C in (1) and (2) together

D in (1) and (2) separately

E in none of the statements

Answer

80   Read the question and decide if you need either both or neither statement in order to answer the question.

Tessa and Catherine weighed themselves at two different occasions. On the first occasion, they weighed 60 kg respectively. How much did they weigh together on the second occasion?

1 On the second occasion Tessa had gained in weight what Catherine had lost in weight in relation to what they weighed on the first occasion.

2 On the second occasion Tessa had gained in absolute weight what Catherine had lost in weight.

There is sufficient information in order to solve the question:

A in (1) but not in (2)

B in (2) but not in (1)

C in (1) and (2) together

D in (1) and (2) separately

E in none of the statements

Answer

81 Read the question and decide if you need either both or neither statement in order to answer the question.

X and Y are two positive whole numbers. What is the number X?

1 75 per cent of X is more than 50 per cent of 20 per cent of Y.

2 150 per cent of X is 75 per cent of 60 per cent of Y.

There is sufficient information in order to solve the question:

A in (1) but not in (2)

B in (2) but not in (1)

C in (1) and (2) together

D in (1) and (2) separately

E in none of the statements

Answer

82 Read the question and decide if you need either both or neither statement in order to answer the question.

There are four bottles of two sizes and different colours on a shelf. One of the bottles, a red one, has been two-thirds filled with water. How many centilitres of water does it contain?

1 When the red bottle is completely filled it contains 50 per cent more than when it is two-thirds filled.

2 The bottles hold either 0.5 or 1.0 litre. When the four bottles are completely filled they altogether hold 3 litres.

There is sufficient information in order to solve the question:

A in (1) but not in (2)

B in (2) but not in (1)

C in (1) and (2) together

D in (1) and (2) separately

E in none of the statements

Answer

83 Read the question and decide if you need either both or neither statement in order to answer the question.

A company rented an aeroplane to transport its employees to a conference. The company had to pay £20,000 to rent the aeroplane independently of how many of the employees actually travelled to the conference. How many employees travelled on the aeroplane to attend the conference?

1 If another 70 employees had travelled on the aeroplane to attend the conference the cost per employee would go down by £18.

2 When the plane flew to the conference 28 per cent of the seats were empty.

There is sufficient information in order to solve the question:

A in (1) but not in (2)

B in (2) but not in (1)

C in (1) and (2) together

D in (1) and (2) separately

E in none of the statements

Answer

84 Read the question and decide if you need either both or neither statement in order to answer the question.

There are 20 equally sized pieces of paper each marked with the numbers 1, 2 or 3 in a box. How many of the pieces of paper are marked with the number 3?

1 The probability of a piece of paper being marked with the number 3 or 1 is 0.6 if taken randomly from the box.

2 There are 12 pieces of paper marked with either 1 or 2.

There is sufficient information in order to solve the question:

A in (1) but not in (2)

B in (2) but not in (1)

C in (1) and (2) together

D in (1) and (2) separately

E in none of the statements

Answer _____

85 Read the question and decide if you need either both or neither statement in order to answer the question.

Index is used to show change over time. The index number for the number of shoes manufactured between 1994 (index = 100) and 1998 rose by 20 units. How many pairs of shoes were manufactured in 1998?

1 There were 224,000 pairs of shoes manufactured in 1996, which was 16,000 pairs less than in 1998.

2 There were 40,000 more pairs of shoes manufactured in 1998 than in 1994.

There is sufficient information in order to solve the question:

A in (1) but not in (2)

B in (2) but not in (1)

C in (1) and (2) together

D in (1) and (2) separately

E in none of the statements

Answer

86 Read the question and decide if you need either both or neither statement in order to answer the question.

There is one red, one blue, one yellow and one green flower-pot on a table. The heaviest of the pots weighs 4 kg. Which colour is the heaviest flowerpot?

1 The blue and the green flowerpots together weigh 2 kg more than the yellow one.

2 The green and the yellow flowerpots together weigh 2 kg more than the red one.

There is sufficient information in order to solve the question:

A in (1) but not in (2)

B in (2) but not in (1)

C in (1) and (2) together

D in (1) and (2) separately

E in none of the statements

Answer

87   Read the question and decide if you need either both or neither statement in order to answer the question.

Out of the starters in a race only a certain number of runners finished, as some abandoned the race. How many of the starters finished the race?

1 If one-third of the runners who finished had instead abandoned and if half of the runners who abandoned the race instead had finished, the number of starting runners who finished the race would have been unchanged.

2 If 30 more runners had finished the race and consequently 30 fewer had abandoned the race, the number of starting runners who finished would increase by 50 per cent.

There is sufficient information in order to solve the question:

A in (1) but not in (2)

B in (2) but not in (1)

C in (1) and (2) together

D in (1) and (2) separately

E in none of the statements

Answer

88   Read the question and decide if you need either both or neither statement in order to answer the question.

Eric picked some apples. Of these, he gave one-third to John, Peter and Andrew. Andrew was given one of the apples. How many apples did Eric pick in total?

1   John gets the most apples, namely half of the apples that Eric gives away plus half an apple.

2   At the point when only John has received his apples, Peter receives half of the apples that remain of the apples that Eric gives away plus half an apple.

There is sufficient information in order to solve the question:

A   in (1) but not in (2)

B   in (2) but not in (1)

C   in (1) and (2) together

D   in (1) and (2) separately

E   in none of the statements

Answer

89 Read the question and decide if you need either both or neither statement in order to answer the question.

A, B, C and D each cut a slice of cake. A took one-third of the cake. How big a part of the cake was left once everyone had taken one slice each?

1 Half of the cake was left when A and B had taken a slice each.

2 B, C and D all had one slice each. Each of these slices was half of the size of A's slice of cake.

There is sufficient information in order to solve the question:

A in (1) but not in (2)

B in (2) but not in (1)

C in (1) and (2) together

D in (1) and (2) separately

E in none of the statements

Answer

90 Read the question and decide if you need either both or neither statement in order to answer the question.

In total, there were 792 men and women participating in a conference. What share of the participants were women?

1 There were 396 fewer men than women participating in the conference.

2 There were three times as many women as men participating in the conference.

There is sufficient information in order to solve the question:

A in (1) but not in (2)

B in (2) but not in (1)

C in (1) and (2) together

D in (1) and (2) separately

E in none of the statements

Answer [   ]

Chapter 7
Mock tests

This chapter comprises four mock tests. The first two require a medium level of numerical skills and familiarity with the vocabulary of business. The second two tests require a medium to high level of competency.

You must decide whether or not this level is suitable for the challenge you face. Do not allow yourself to be discouraged if you find these tests too difficult. It may be that you do not face a test at this level; alternatively, undertake more practice.

Mock test 1

Data interpretation

This mock test comprises 30 multiple choice questions. They require you to interpret information from tables and graphs and use the information to answer the questions.

Allow yourself 20 minutes to complete the test.

Answers and explanations are provided in Part Three.

TABLE 7.1 The market demand and supply of potatoes

Price of potatoes (pence per kg)	Total market demand (tonnes)	Total market supply (tonnes)
4	700	100
8	500	200
12	350	350
16	200	530
20	100	700

1   How many potatoes would be demanded if the price per kg were 16p?

A   B   C   D
200   350   500   100

Answer [   ]

2   If the price per kg of potatoes were 4p, how many tonnes would be supplied by the market?

A   B   C   D
700   350   100   200

Answer [   ]

3   If the price of potatoes were to rise from 8p to 12p per kg, what effect would this have on the demand?

A Increase by 350 tonnes
B Decrease by 350 tonnes
C Increase by 150 tonnes
D Decrease by 150 tonnes

Answer [   ]

4   What is the equilibrium price in this market?

A   B   C   D
4p   8p   12p   16p

Answer [   ]

5   If the price of potatoes were set at 8p per kg by the government, what would be the effect on the market?

A Shortage of 300 tonnes
B Surplus of 300 tonnes
C Shortage of 500 tonnes
D Surplus of 200 tonnes

Answer

6   How much more surplus would be created if the price rose from 16p to 20p per kg of potatoes?

A	B	C	D
700 tonnes	530 tonnes	350 tonnes	270 tonnes

Answer

A comparison of economic growth between 1953 and 1963

Average Growth Rate (%)

□ Average Growth Rates 1953–58
▣ Average Growth Rates 1958–63

Countries

7   What is the average growth rate for the UK between 1953 and 1958?

A	B	C	D
1%	2%	3%	4%

Answer

8   Which country had the highest average growth rate between 1958 and 1963?

A	B	C	D
Japan	West Germany	Italy	France

Answer

9 In which country is the average growth rate for 1953–58 greater than the one for 1958–63?

A	B	C	D
UK	USA	France	West Germany

Answer [   ]

10 Which country experiences the largest rise in average growth rate?

A	B	C	D
France	Italy	West Germany	Japan

Answer [   ]

TABLE 7.2 Sales of 'Outrage' outerwear for the years 1992–94 (given quarterly)

Year	Quarter	Sales revenue (£)
1992	1	256
	2	220
	3	130
	4	283
1993	1	260
	2	225
	3	137
	4	288
1994	1	264
	2	227
	3	141
	4	290

11 Which quarter is constantly more profitable for the company?

A	B	C	D
1	2	3	4

Answer [   ]

12 In which quarter of 1993 is the sales revenue the lowest?

A	B	C	D
1	2	3	4

Answer [   ]

13 Calculate the mean for the sales revenue during 1994.

A	B	C	D
230.5	227.5	222.5	212.5

Answer [   ]

14 In which year does the company experience the largest range of sales revenue?

A	B	C
1992	1993	1994

Answer [   ]

15 What is the median of sales revenue in 1992?

A	B	C	D
238	240	242	244

Answer [   ]

TABLE 7.3 Rainfall, sunshine, and wind speed for Italy throughout 1998

	Rainfall (in mm)	Sunshine (in hours)	Wind speed (in knots)
January	113	56	18
February	140	86	14
March	160	130	25
April	91	140	28
May	78	155	12
June	63	158	14
July	70	230	7
August	75	210	16
September	101	195	18
October	104	145	20
November	140	93	16
December	137	75	14

16   What is the arithmetic mean of the rainfall in 1998?

A	B	C	D
100 mm	106 mm	112 mm	118 mm

Answer _____

17   Which month had approximately six days' worth of sunshine?

A	B	C	D
September	October	November	December

Answer _____

18   By what percentage did the wind speed decrease between October and November?

A	B	C	D
10%	20%	30%	40%

Answer _____

19 Which month's sunshine is over four times less than July's?

A	B	C	D
January	February	March	April

Answer [   ]

20 How many months experienced over 12,500 minutes of sunshine?

A	B	C	D
1	2	3	4

Answer [   ]

TABLE 7.4 Private higher education institutions in Central and Eastern Europe

	Number of institutions	Number of students	Typical annual fees (in $)
Armenia	69	20000	300
Azerbaijan	17	3800	500–1500
Bulgaria	9	27900	375–570
Czech Rep	8	2900	1210–1340
Estonia	24	13300	1640
Hungary	32	28000	800–4800
Latvia	13	14600	1050
Lithuania	7	1300	2500
Moldova	39	3900	155–620
Poland	195	37770	440–910
Romania	54	130100	210
Slovakia	2	2000	800–1200
Slovenia	11	2900	2340–7020

21 What is the average number of students attending a single institution in Moldova?

A	B	C	D
0.01	10	100	1,000

Answer [   ]

22   If the Lithuanian government considers the 'ideal' institution to have just 100 students, how many new institutions should be opened up according to them?

A	B	C	D
0	2	4	6

Answer [   ]

23   What country has the biggest range of annual fees?

A	B	C	D
Bulgaria	Czech Republic	Hungary	Slovenia

Answer [   ]

24   Given that the institutions give their entire income to the government, which government is receiving the most?

A	B	C	D
Armenian	Estonian	Lithuanian	Romanian

Answer [   ]

25   What is the minimum that each institution in Hungary receives from its students?

A	B	C	D
700,000	2,450,000	4,200,000	78,400,000

Answer [   ]

26   The Latvian government imposes a 6 per cent rise on all annual tuition fees. How much will the institutions be gaining or losing in total, if this increase causes the number of students to drop by 2 per cent?

A gaining 594,804
B losing 594,804
C gaining 919,800
D losing 919,800

Answer [   ]

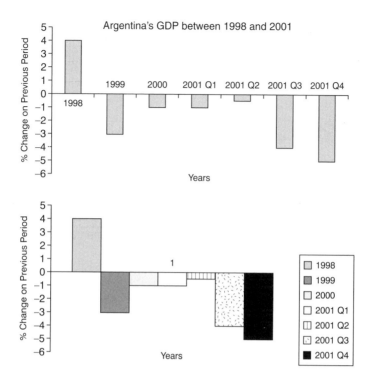

27   What happened to Argentina's GDP between 1997 and 1998?

A Increased 4 per cent

B Decreased 4 per cent

C Remained stable

D Cannot tell

Answer ⬚

28   Given that Argentina's GDP was $500 million in 1998, what was it in 1999?

A	B	C	D
$480 million	$485 million	$515 million	$520 million

Answer ⬚

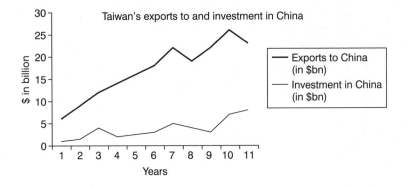

29   Which is the only year in which Taiwan experienced a peak both in its exports to China and in its investments in China?

A	B	C	D
3	7	9	11

Answer [   ]

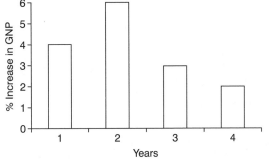

30   In which year was Country X's GNP the highest?

A	B	C	D
1	2	3	4

Answer [   ]

End of test.

Mock test 2

Business judgement

This mock test comprises 39 multiple choice questions. They require you to demonstrate a comprehension of business practice and interpret financial information from tables and graphs, using the information to answer the questions.

Allow yourself 40 minutes to complete the test.

1 Which of the following terms is an example of cash outflow?

A	B	C	D
Employee insurance	Sales revenue	Bank loan	Tax refund

Answer [　　　　　]

2 What is the price of one currency relative to another currency?

A	B	C	D
Comparison	Inflation	Exchange rate	Exercise price

Answer [　　　　　]

3 What is the ownership interest of shareholders in a company?

A	B	C	D
Economic value	Equity	Exponential value	Economic profit

Answer [　　　　　]

4 How are cash payments made to shareholders of a firm referred to as?

A	B	C	D
Dividends	Excess returns	Repayments	Abnormal profits

Answer [　　　　　]

5   What is nominal value more frequently referred to as?

A	B	C	D
Interest value	Net value	Marginal value	Face value

Answer [   ]

6   What shows the financial flows as and when they actually happen?

A   Profit and loss account
B   Balance sheet
C   Cash flow
D   Forecast

Answer [   ]

7   In what period are transactions recorded in profit and loss accounts?

A   Period preceding the period to which they relate
B   Period to which they relate
C   Period following the period to which they relate
D   Period in which they were paid

Answer [   ]

8   What can be considered to be a snapshot of a company's finances at one moment in time, for example 31 December 2000?

A   Balance sheet
B   Credit sheet
C   Capital outlays
D   Assets assessment

Answer [   ]

9   Which of the following definitions describes normal profit?

A   Firm can only just cover its variable costs
B   Opportunity cost of being in business

C Excess of total profit
D Firm can cover all its costs

Answer

10 Which of the following is a cash inflow?

A	B	C	D
Bank loan	Bank repayment	Expenditure	Depreciation

Answer

TABLE 7.5 Cash flow 1 for small company in 2001

Expenditure (in £)	Jan	Feb	Mar	Apr	May	Jun	Jul	Aug	Sep	Oct	Nov	Dec
5 Salaries	0	0	0	0	0	0	600	800	1000	1200	1400	1600
6 Professional fees	800	800	800	800	900	900	800	800	800	800	800	800

Using the above table answer the following:

11 Is the total expenditure greater for professional fees or for salaries? *Answer*

12 By what percentage do salaries increase between August and September? *Answer*

13 Does the percentage increase in salaries between September and October remain the same, decrease, or increase compared to August–September's increase?

Answer

14 Calculate the National Insurance payment that the company will have to sustain in 2001, considering that NI is 5 per cent of salaries.

Answer

TABLE 7.6 Cash flow 2 for Bella in 1996

Income (in $)													
Nos	Jan	Feb	Mar	Apr	May	Jun	Jul	Aug	Sep	Oct	Nov	Dec	Total
1 Opening	0												0
2 Director's	?		'										?
3 Other	80000												80000
4 Sales	0	1000	2000	2500	3000	4000	3500	3000	?	4500	6000	7000	41000
A Total	90000	1000	2000	2500	3000	4000	3500	3000	?	4500	6000	7000	131000

TABLE 7.7 Profit and loss account, for Big Bikes (first six months)

	Month 1	Month 2	Month 3	Month 4	Month 5	Month 6	H1
Sales (in $)	0	20000	0	40000	0	50000	110000
Costs of sales	0	13600	0	27200	0	33900	74700
Operating costs (in $)							
Administration costs	25800	27100	27100	28400	28400	29100	165900
Other expenditure	12500	33800	25200	17200	16500	18700	123900

Using Table 7.6 answer the following:

15 In which month do the sales double
   from the previous month?   *Answer* _____

16 How much must the director loan the firm, in order for the total
   income to be £131,000?

                                     Answer _____

Using Table 7.7 answer the following:

17 What are the total costs for month 2?

                                     Answer _____

18 Which month yields the
   greatest gross profit?   *Answer* _____

19 Which month has the greatest
   operating costs?   *Answer* _____

Business comprehension

Passage 1

The number of people receiving unemployment benefit in Britain
grew by 4,800 in November, the first time since 1992 that the number
of claimants has grown for two straight months. Inflation waned in
November, as consumer-prices grew by a modest 0.9 per cent, the
lowest level since July 1963. British retail sales surged by 7.1 per
cent in volume terms in the year to November, the biggest increase
since mid-1988.

20 The number of people unemployed in Britain was 4,800 in the
   month of November.

   A   B   C
   True   False   Cannot tell

                                     Answer _____

21   What happened to inflation during November?

A   B   C
Declined   Rose   Remained stable

Answer [_____]

22   If the price of a consumer good was £100 at the beginning of November, how much did it cost at the end of the month?

A   B   C   D
£99.10   £100.90   £109.00   £190.00

Answer [_____]

Passage 2

The body mass index (BMI) is the ratio of a person's weight (in kilograms) to the square of his height (in metres). Obesity, defined as a BMI of more than 30, is a growing problem in many OECD countries, especially English-speaking ones. In 1999, 20 per cent of Britons were obese, compared with 7 per cent in 1980. The United States, though, has the biggest share of obese people: more than one-fifth of its citizens weigh in with a BMI of 30-plus.

23   The article states that more than 15 per cent of Americans are obese.

A   B   C
True   False   Cannot tell

Answer [_____]

24   What is the correct formula for calculating the BMI of a person who weighs 55 kilograms and is 1.65 metres tall?

A $55 + (1.65)^2$
B $55 * (1.65)^2$
C $55 / (1.65)^2$
D None of the above

Answer [_____]

25 Given that the population of Great Britain in 1999 was 59.8 million, how many Britons were obese in 1999?

A	B	C	D
11,196	119,600	1,196,000	11,960,000

Answer [　　　　　]

26 What happened to the percentage of obese people in Britain between 1980 and 1999?

A More than doubled
B More than tripled
C Cannot tell

Answer [　　　　　]

Passage 3

The biggest figure alongside Mr Rutelli in the opposition is Piero Fassino, the new leader of the ex-communist Democrats of the Left. Mr Fassino will struggle to rejuvenate his party. Since 1996 its tally of votes has dipped from 21 per cent to under 17 per cent; in the early 1980s, it got 30 per cent. Meanwhile, Mr Rutelli's own clutch of parties on the centre-left, known as the Margherita (Daisy), shot up at the last election to win nearly 15 per cent of the votes cast.

27 Mr Rutelli and Piero Fassino are both opposition MPs and opponents.

A	B	C
True	False	Cannot tell

Answer [　　　　　]

28 Mr Fassino will fight to restore the ex-communist Democrats.

A	B	C
True	False	Cannot tell

Answer [　　　　　]

29 The number of votes for Fassino's party has fallen every year between 1980 and 1996.

A	B	C
True	False	Cannot tell

Answer [   ]

30 If the votes cast at the last election were 10 million, how many did the Margherita nearly receive?

A	B	C	D
15,000	150,000	1,500,000	15,000,000

Answer [   ]

Passage 4

Your survey of European business and the euro (December 1st) aptly illustrates that the euro is primarily about politics and not economics. Enthusiasts claim that the euro will provide many benefits to businesses and consumers, and frequently cite reduced transaction costs as an example. But even after notes and coins are introduced there will be no automatic reduction in such costs.

31 The euro is only about politics.

A	B	C
True	False	Cannot tell

Answer [   ]

32 How can you describe the writer of this article?

A Favours the euro
B Against the euro
C Cannot tell

Answer [   ]

Passage 5

Microsoft appealed against a judgment ordering it to be split in two for acting as an illegal monopolist. The appeals court rejected the

break-up, but upheld the finding that Microsoft had broken the law.
A new judge ordered Microsoft to propose alternative punishment.

33 In the end, Microsoft was not found guilty of acting as a
monopoly.

A	B	C
True	False	Cannot tell

Answer [   ]

Passage 6

Recession turned to slump in Argentina, after the government imposed
budget cuts and then bank controls as it battled against default on
its $135 billion public debt and to retain its fixed exchange rate.

34 Argentina is suffering more as a result of its public debt rather
than due to its fixed exchange rate.

A	B	C
True	False	Cannot tell

Answer [   ]

Business finance

TABLE 7.8 Extract of balance sheet for Firm X (31/12/06)

Fixed assets (at cost)	£
Freehold property (at cost)	60100
Plant & machinery (at cost)	32640
Depreciation	(12840)
Small machine	1600
Total fixed assets	81500
Current assets	£
Debtors	14000
Stocks	6000
Miscellaneous	375
Total current assets	20375
Current liabilities	...

35 What does the £14,000 on the 'Debtors' row represent?

A Money firm X owes

B Money firm X is owed

C Money firm X has to pay as dividend

D Money firm X received as debts

Answer

36 What would the total fixed assets be without considering depreciation?

A	B	C	D
£68,660	£81,500	£94,340	Cannot tell

Answer

37 What is the ratio of total fixed assets to total current assets?

A	B	C	D
1:2	2:1	1:4	4:1

Answer

38 What asset has exactly 16 times the value of 'Miscellaneous'?

A	B	C	D
Freehold property	Small machine	Debtors	Stocks

Answer

39 Which of the following could be found under the 'Liabilities' heading?

A	B	C	D
Bank loan	Cash at bank	Inventory	Capital

Answer

End of test.

Mock test 3

Business judgement

This mock test comprises 13 multiple choice questions. It requires you to demonstrate a medium to high comprehension of business practice and to interpret financial information from tables, using the information to answer the questions.

Allow yourself 30 minutes to complete the test.

Using the Table on pages 130–31 answer the following:

1   How is row C (ie Monthly + or –)
calculated?   *Answer*   [   ]

2   What is the total expenditure paid
in the month of May?   *Answer*   [   ]

3   What two cells (being equal) indicate that the cash flow has been calculated correctly?

Answer   [   ]

4   What happens to the percentage of 'Direct costs' between the months of May and June?

A Drops by 12.5%

B Increases by 12.5%

C Stays the same

Answer   [   ]

5   What percentage of December's total expenditure is made up of Transport costs? Calculate to the nearest integer.

A	B	C	D	E
1%	2%	3%	4%	5%

Answer   [   ]

TABLE 7.9 Cash flow for Company Z in 2007

Nos	Jan	Feb	Mar	Apr	May	Jun	Jul	Aug	Sep	Oct	Nov	Dec	Total
Income													
1 Opening balance	0												0
2 Other loans	80000												80000
3 Sales	0	1000	2000	2500	3000	4000	3500	3000	4500	4500	6000	7000	41000
A Total income	80000	1000	2000	2500	3000	4000	3500	3000	4500	4500	6000	7000	121000
Expenditure													
4 Wages	1000	1000	1000	1000	1000	1000	1000	1000	1000	1000	1500	1500	13000
5 Salaries	1500	1500	1500	1500	1500	1500	1500	1500	1500	1500	1500	1500	18000
6 NI (at 5%)	125	125	125	125	125	125	125	125	125	125	150	150	1550
7 Direct costs (at 40%)	400	800	1000	1200	1600	1400	1200	1800	1800	2400	2800	600	17000
8 Marketing/Sales	2000	2000	2000	1000	1000	500	500	500	1000	1500	1500	1500	15000
9 Utilities	0	0	350	0	0	290	0	0	220	0	0	390	1250
10 Telephone	100	0	0	200	0	0	250	0	0	290	0	0	840
11 Office expenses	700	400	200	200	200	200	200	200	200	200	500	700	3900
12 Computer & fax	2000	0	0	0	0	0	0	0	0	0	0	0	2000
13 Transport	200	200	200	200	200	200	200	200	200	200	200	200	2400

TABLE 7.9 Continued

Nos	Jan	Feb	Mar	Apr	May	Jun	Jul	Aug	Sep	Oct	Nov	Dec	Total
14 Travel	40	40	40	60	60	60	40	40	60	60	60	60	620
15 Rent	3000	0	0	3000	0	0	3000	0	0	3000	0	0	12000
16 Business rates	0	300	0	0	300	0	0	300	0	0	300	0	1200
17 Professional fees	2000	0	0	0	0	0	0	0	0	0	0	0	2000
18 Start-up costs	2000	0	0	0	0	0	0	0	0	0	0	0	2000
B Total expenditure	15065	6365	6415	8485	5985	5275	8015	5665	6105	10275	8510	6600	92760
C Monthly + or –	64935	–5365	–4415	–5985	–2985	–1275	–4515	–2665	–1605	–5775	–2510	400	28240
D Cash flow	64935	59570	55155	49170	46185	44910	40395	37730	36125	30350	27840	28240	28240

TABLE 7.10 X's savings and income

Month	Savings (in £)	Income (in £)
January	100	1000
February	200	2200
March	300	3300
April	400	4400
May	500	5500
June	600	6600
July	700	7700

6 What is the average propensity to save (aps) in the month of January?

A	B	C	D
0.001	0.01	0.1	10

Answer [ ]

7 In how many months is the average propensity to save equal?

A	B	C	D
None	Two	Four	Six

Answer [ ]

8 Given that the marginal propensity to save (mps) is 0.2, if the total income rises by £400, by how much will savings be increased?

A	B	C	D
£20	£40	£60	£80

Answer [ ]

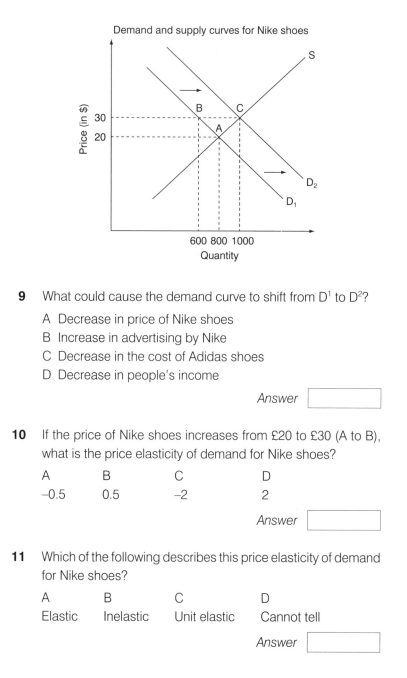

Demand and supply curves for Nike shoes

9   What could cause the demand curve to shift from D¹ to D²?

A   Decrease in price of Nike shoes
B   Increase in advertising by Nike
C   Decrease in the cost of Adidas shoes
D   Decrease in people's income

Answer

10   If the price of Nike shoes increases from £20 to £30 (A to B), what is the price elasticity of demand for Nike shoes?

A	B	C	D
−0.5	0.5	−2	2

Answer

11   Which of the following describes this price elasticity of demand for Nike shoes?

A	B	C	D
Elastic	Inelastic	Unit elastic	Cannot tell

Answer

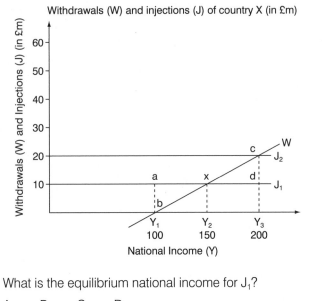

Withdrawals (W) and injections (J) of country X (in £m)

12   What is the equilibrium national income for J_1?

A   B   C   D
Y_1 Y_2 Y_3 Cannot be determined

Answer [   ]

13   Given that injections shift from £10 million to £20 million, calculate the multiplier.

A   B   C   D
0.2   2   5   10

Answer [   ]

End of test.

Mock test 4

Data sufficiency

This sort of question does not require you to answer the question but simply identify which information is required in order to answer it or to state whether or not it can be answered.

This test comprises 34 questions; allow yourself 60 minutes in which to attempt all of them. The bulk of this time should be committed to the first part of the test. It demands a medium to high level of numerical competency.

Answers and explanations are provided in Part Three.

Part 1

Passage 1: There is a straight line passing through the origin and two points, A and B. Point A is (3,6), whereas the other is unknown. The line is 20 cm long.

1   Which of the following is needed in order to calculate the slope of this line?

A Coordinates of point B
B Intercept on the y-axis
C Constants of the line's equation
D No further information is needed

Answer ⬚

Passage 2: A nightclub called Balance has a capacity of 360 people. The entrance costs £18 for men. Women enter for one-third of that price. Balance reaches full capacity on Thursday, Friday and Saturday nights. The remaining days of the week Balance reaches only one-third of its full capacity.

2   You are asked to calculate Balance's revenue for one night. Which of the following gives you just enough information to solve this problem?

A Day of the week
B Day of the week, number of men
C Day of the week, number of women,
   and women's entrance price
D Day of the week, number of men,
   and relevant costs

Answer ⬚

Passage 3: The symbol § represents one of the following operations: addition, subtraction, multiplication, or division.

3 In order to determine only one value for 4 § 2, which of the following would you need to be given?

A   B   C
0 § 1 = 1   1 § 0 = 1   1 § 1 = 1

Answer [   ]

Passage 4: What is the value of x in △ABC if the triangle is an isosceles triangle and x is the angle with the highest value?

4 With which of the following information is it possible to answer this question?

A AB = AC
B second angle, $y = 44$
C Both A and B

Answer [   ]

Passage 5: Andy Stanton is a real-estate agent. He recently sold a house and received a commission of 5 per cent of the selling price. He willingly gave half of his earnings to his friend, Mike, who had helped him conclude the deal.

5 With which of the following information is it possible to determine the selling price of the house Andy sold?

A Selling price is two-thirds of the original purchase price
B Selling price – Andy's commission = £76,000
C Selling price was 150 per cent of the original purchase price of £44,000
D Mike's earnings from the deal = £10,000

Answer [   ]

Passage 6: Given the following triangle, and knowing that the area of a triangle can be found using: ½ab sin C answer question 6.

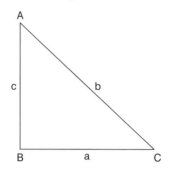

6   Which of the following information is needed to calculate triangle ABC's area?

A	B	C
a and b	b and c	a and C

Answer [   ]

Passage 7: Given the following circle, where *r* is the radius, A is an angle, and *a* is the length of the arc, calculate its circumference and area.

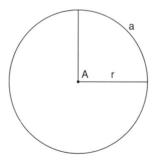

7   What information is needed in order to answer the above question?

A Circle's radian
B Circle's diameter
C Length of the arc
D Degree of angle A

Answer [   ]

Passage 8: Your grandparents invest £200 in your name on your 18th birthday, to be paid to you on your 21st birthday. You will also receive the interest earned at 12½ per cent per annum.

8   What further information do you need, in order to calculate how much you will receive?

A Number of years of investment
B Percentage rate per time period
C Both of the above
D None

Answer _____

Passage 9: A total of *t* people use three ways of transportation to go to work in year *n*. *X* represents the number of people that use the car. *Y* represents the number of people that use the train. *Z* represents the number of people that use the bus. *W* represents the number of people that use none of the above ways of transportation and that walk to work.

How many people use both the bus and the train only to go to work in year *n*?

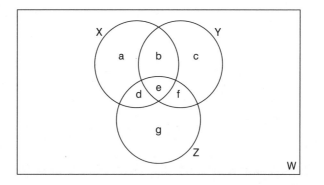

9   With which of the following information *alone* could you answer this question?

A Value of *e*   B Values of *c* and *g*
C Value of *f*   D Value of *b* and *d*

Answer _____

10 Still referring to Passage 9, what information would be needed in order to determine the number of people that use the car or the train to go to work in year n?

A $Z = 10,000$ and $X + Y + Z = 50,000$
B $X = 25,000$ and $X + Y + Z = 60,000$
C $X = 25,000$ and $Y = 3X$
D $Z = 15,000$ and $Y = 2Z$

Answer [   ]

Passage 10: Mary is twice the height of Ben. Ben is three times the height of Jack. David is the same height as Mary. How tall is Jack?

11 Which of the following statements is true?

A With Mary's height alone, it's possible to calculate Jack's height.

B With Ben's height alone, it's possible to calculate Jack's height.

C With David's height alone, it's possible to calculate Jack's height.

D Both Mary's and Ben's height are needed to calculate Jack's height.

Answer [   ]

Passage 11: The probability of passing the Chemistry final exam is 1 in 20, whereas the probability of failing the Biology final exam is x. Alice is a student who wants to take the easier science class (ie the one with the easier final exam to pass).

12 What is the only extra information that Alice needs in order to decide which science class to take?

A Probability of failing Chemistry final exam

B Probability of passing Chemistry final exam

C Probability of passing Biology final exam

D Probability of passing Biology final exam and probability of passing Chemistry final exam

Answer [   ]

Passage 12: The following set of data is given:

12, 2, 2, 8, x, 4

and it is given that $8 < x < 12$.

13 With the given data, which of the following is it possible to calculate?

A	B	C	D
Range	Mode	Mean	Median

Answer [   ]

Passage 13: The base-weighted price index is calculated as follows:

$$\frac{\text{Total cost of base-year quantities at current prices}}{\text{Total cost of base-year quantities at base-year prices}}$$

Calculate the base-weighted price index of the following:

The price (in pence) for the three commodities being consumed in Country X are represented below, together with the amounts of each consumed. 1992 is the current year, whereas 1991 is the base-year.

TABLE 7.11

Year	1991		1992	
	Price (p_0)	quantity (q_0)	price (p_n)	quantity (q^n)
Fish (per pound)	240	20	290	25
Potatoes (per pound)	w	x	y	z
Milk (per pint)	27	200	29	190

14 Which of the following are needed in order to calculate the base-weighted price index?

A	B	C	D
w	x	y	z

Answer [   ]

Passage 14: The standard deviation is calculated with the following formula:

$$\sqrt{\frac{\Sigma(x - \bar{x})^2}{\text{No. of Items}}}$$

15   Which of the following is needed to calculate the standard deviation?

A x

B mean of x

C number of items

D all of the above

Answer ⎕

Passage 15: Probability of A and B = P (A) * P (B).

Series of Statements:

1 P (A) = ¼

2 P (B) = ½

3 P (A) or P (B) = ¾

4 P (A) / P (B) = ½

16   Which of the following statements is true?

A Possible to calculate Prob. of A and B with statement #1 alone.

B Possible to calculate Prob. of A and B with statement #1 and #2.

C Possible to calculate Prob. of A and B with statement #1 and #3.

D Possible to calculate Prob. of A and B with statement #2 and #4.

Answer ⎕

Part 2

Statement 1: Germany used to be the economic powerhouse of Europe. Today it is a drag. The economy shrank in the third quarter of the last year, and probably in the fourth too, pushing growth down to about 0.7 per cent, the lowest in the EU, with little better expected next year. Nor can the government afford to throw Keynesian money at the problem: the budget deficit is perilously close to the 3 per cent limit set for members of the euro-zone.

17   Germany has been experiencing low growth in its economy.

A	B	C
True	False	Cannot tell

Answer [   ]

18   Germany is the only EU country to have had economic problems this year.

A	B	C
True	False	Cannot tell

Answer [   ]

19   Italy's growth rate this year was not less than Germany's 0.7 per cent.

A	B	C
True	False	Cannot tell

Answer [   ]

20   Germany's budget deficit is higher than all the other members of the euro-zone.

A	B	C
True	False	Cannot tell

Answer [   ]

Statement 2: The value of global merger and acquisition activity in 2001 was $1.6 trillion, half what it was worth the previous year, according to data from Dealogic. In 2000, the inflated value of high-tech shares fuelled many a deal that now looks unwise.

21 According to Dealogic, the value of global merger and acquisition activity in 2000 was $8 billion.

A   B   C
True   False   Cannot tell

Answer

22 The value of the high-tech shares in 2000 was raised artificially.

A   B   C
True   False   Cannot tell

Answer

Statement 3: Five German banks felt the wrath of the European Commission. In its latest round of cartel-busting, the commission levied fines of $100 million (£90.4 million) for fixing commissions on the exchange of the 12 euro-area currencies since 1997. Three banks said they would appeal.

23 60 per cent of the German banks fined are planning to appeal.

A   B   C
True   False   Cannot tell

Answer

24 The $1 is equal to £0.904.

A   B   C
True   False   Cannot tell

Answer

Statement 4: Telekomunikacja Polska announced that it would get rid of 12,000 employees next year, 20 per cent of its workforce. France Telecom, which acquired 35 per cent of the former state monopoly from the Polish government last year, had said that job cuts would come but had agreed with powerful unions that it would wait four years.

25 Telekomunikacja Polska currently has 60,000 employees.

A	B	C
True	False	Cannot tell

Answer [   ]

Statement 5: In 1994, Arizona's voters passed a proposition, similar to the one in California, that raised cigarette taxes and used the revenue to fund a successful comprehensive tobacco education and control programme. Since 1996, this programme has resulted in a 22.6 per cent decrease in adult smokers, a 23.3 per cent fall in high-school smoking, and a 39 per cent drop in middle-school smoking.

26 This programme has had the least effect on adult smokers.

A	B	C
True	False	Cannot tell

Answer [   ]

27 This programme has succeeded in cutting smoking by just over 85 per cent.

A	B	C
True	False	Cannot tell

Answer [   ]

28 This programme had more success in California.

A	B	C
True	False	Cannot tell

Answer [   ]

29 There is more high-school smoking in Arizona than there is in middle schools.

A   B   C
True   False   Cannot tell

Answer [   ]

Statement 6: Between 1960 and 1995, life expectancy in poor countries rose by 22 years, largely because modern medicine prevented millions of premature deaths. In the 1950s, 16 per cent of children died before their fifth birthday; now only 4 per cent do.

30 Children now are four times less likely to die before their fifth birthday than they were in the 1950s.

A   B   C
True   False   Cannot tell

Answer [   ]

Statement 7: While Argentina was stuck in its fixed-currency straitjacket, the floating *real* has helped ease worries about Brazil's current-account gap, making its exports more competitive and imports more expensive. After six years of trade deficits, Brazil enjoyed a surplus of around $2.6 billion in 2001.

31 In 1996, Brazil had a trade deficit.

A   B   C
True   False   Cannot tell

Answer [   ]

32 The increase in the Brazilian exports' competitiveness, due to Argentina's fixed-currency, helped Brazil enjoy a surplus in 2001.

A   B   C
True   False   Cannot tell

Answer [   ]

Statement 8: Bankruptcies and lay-offs continue to take their toll in Japan. Unemployment rose to a record high of 5.5 per cent in November, up from 4.5 per cent in October: 3.5 million workers are now without jobs. Japanese industrial production plunged by 13.2 per cent in the last 12 months, sliding to its lowest level in 14 years. Deflation continued, with consumer prices falling by 1.0 per cent over the year to November.

33   Japan's unemployment rose by 5.5 per cent in November.

A   B   C
True   False   Cannot tell

Answer ☐

34   Japanese industrial production has fallen on average by 1.1 per cent each month for the last 12 months.

A   B   C
True   False   Cannot tell

Answer ☐

End of test.

Part Three
Answers and many detailed explanations

Answers and explanations

Chapter 3 Quantitative reasoning

1 3,530 JPY (40 × 88.25 = 3,530)

2 4.4 (200 × 0.022 = 4.4)

3 B, 1 ZAR: 0.0846 GBP (inverse means the opposite so you must find the ZAR = GBP rate. Find this by dividing 1 by 11.82 and the closest suggested answer to this value is B, 0.0846)

4

1/2	0.50	50%
3/4	0.75	75%
1/5	0.20	20%
3/5	0.60	60%
3/8	0.375	37.5%
1/4	0.25	25%

5 C, the middle number

6 The value of integer *W* is between 50 and 99 (note that in this instance *W* cannot equal 100 but can equal 50)

7   Less than or equal to

8   Less than

9   Greater than

10 C, reasonable positive correlation (a stronger correlation would form a straighter line on the graph)

11 9/20

12 11/20

13 45% and 0.45

14 10.5 (63 divided by 6)

15 Median = 11 (13 + 9 divided by 2), Range = 17 (19 – 2)

16 A and D, 35 and 30

17 HH, TT, TH, HT (where H = heads and T = tails in all order)

18 1/12 (P (A + B) = P(A) $\times$ P(B) = 1/2 $\times$ 1/6 = 1/12)

19 A, the same

20 E, all of these

21 729 (learn the first few powers up to 10 in the same way as you learnt your multiplication tables)

22 64 (learn the basic cubed values)

23 2 to the power of 4

24 5 m (Area = X^2 = 25 m^2, X = $\sqrt{25}$, so X = 5 m)

25 A, $d = 2r$

26 22/7

27 C–B (angles with arrows pointing in an anticlockwise direction are positive while those pointing in a clockwise direction are negative)

28 F, 6 (they are 1, 2, 4, 8, 16, 32. A common factor of a number is a number that divides into it without remainder. 1 and 32 are trivial)

29 8 (highest common factor is highest number which divides exactly)

30 1 and 13

31 A prime number (a number that has only 1 and itself as common factors – you should learn the first 10)

32 3 (they are 5, 7 and 17)

33 D, 8 (they are 2, 3, 4, 6, 8, 12, 16, 24)

34 18

35 E, 8 (don't confuse this with $2 \times 3 = 6$; it is in fact $2 \times 2 \times 2 = 8$)

36 32

37 81

38 B, 81 divided by 9

39 C, 2 to the power of 4×2 to the power of 5

40 40,079 km (double the radius to get the diameter and then multiply it by π approximated as 3.142)

41

5%	0.05
17.5%	0.175
25%	0.25
150%	1.5
0.5%	0.005

42 20% ($117/565 = 1/5 = 0.2 = 20\%$)

43 35% ($126/360 = 0.35 = 35\%$)

44 40%

45 20% and 15% ($56/280 = 0.2 = 20\%$, $42/280 = 0.15 = 15\%$)

46 70% ($301/430 = 0.7 = 70\%$)

47 105.75 ($90 + (90 \times 0.175) = 105.75$)

48 97.75 ($85 + (85 \times 0.15) = 97.75$)

49 24 ($15 + (15 \times 0.60) = 24$)

50 106.4 ($140 - (140 \times 0.24) = 140 - 33.6 = 106.4$)

51 50.4 ($63 - (63 \times 0.20) = 63 - 12.6 = 50.4$)

52 13.14 ($73 - (73 \times 0.82) = 73 - 59.86 = 13.14$)

53 250 ($1.2X = 300$)

54 375 ($1.12X = 420$)

55 430 ($1.5X = 645$)

56 1:6

57 2:13 (divide both by HCF which is 30)

58 3:14 (divide both by HCF which is 25)

59 1:7 (HCF 9)

60 5:13 (HCF 19)

61 21:42

62 44:66:22

63 £4.50, £3.50, £4.00

64 $x = 7$ (add 3 each side to give $3x = 21$)

65 $x = 9$ (change to $(x + 6) = 75/5$, which simplifies to $x + 6 = 15$, so $x = 9$)

66 $-5\ 1/3$ (subtract $3x$ from each side and subtract 10 from each side to give: $3x = -16$)

67 $6\ 3/4$ (expand brackets to give $2x + 18 = 6x - 9$, add 9 to give $2x + 27 = 6x$ then minus $2x$ to get $27 = 4x$

68 $X = -4$ (remove fractions by multiplying by 8 which gives $4(x + 2) = 1(3x + 4)$, expand brackets to give $4x + 8 = 3x + 4$, minus $3x$ to give $x + 8 = 4$)

69 Because when plotted on a graph they form a straight line

70 $Y \propto x$

71 $Y \propto \sqrt{x}$

72 $Y \propto x^2$

73 D–E (distance is equal), A–B (distance increases steadily), B–C (distance is decreasing)

74 1,500 ($1/10 \times P = 150$)

75 2 to the power of 5 (every two hours the new total will double)

76 Every year the currency will have 0.98 times the value of the year before, so after four years it will have 0.98^4 times the original value. For a small percentage and a small number of years this is approximately equal to subtracting the percentage decrease each year, ie 2% per year over four years is approximately equal to 8% over four years

77 C, 1 gm

78 5,712 (each year the new total increases by 30%)

79 Four years

80 The 70–79 group (group 7). Make sure that you revise frequency tables; they are a common business tool

81 65 (there are 16 entries so it is between the 8 and 9 results which are both 65)

82 10, 11.7, 11.7 ($5 + 10 + 15 = 30$ divided by $3 = 10$, $10 + 15 + 10 = 35$ divided by $3 = 11.7$, $15 + 10 + 10 = 35$ divided by $3 = 11.7$. Moving averages are used in the deduction of trends from data)

83 75:100:25 (total sample 200)

84 2, inter-quartile range (this method ensures that the effect of any skew (positive or negative) is limited to the relevant quartile)

85 C, 1 in 4

86 C, 1 (probability is measured on a scale of 0 to 1)

87 C, 600 cm^2 (there are six surfaces each with a surface area of 100 cm^2)

88 E, 23 (2^4 = 16. 16 − 9 + 16 = 23)

89 C, 187.5 cm^3 (the top of the shape is half of the volume of the bottom half, so volume is 5 × 5 × 5 × 1.5 = 125 × 1.5

90 A, 31 (it is a sequence of prime numbers)

91 B, 4x (x^2 cancels from top and bottom leaving 4x)

92 C, 48% (80% set off, 80% of those do not break down and 75% of those arrive on time. Total therefore = 0.8 × 0.8 × 0.75 = 0.48 or 48%)

93 C, 10 To get between the first and second numbers in the sequence you add 2. To get between the sixth and seventh you add 7. Following this rule, sometimes called a triangular sequence, gives the following: 1, 3, 6, 10, 15, 21, 28

94 E, 12:1 (there are 2 × 6 × blue blocks for each green block)

95 E, £13,310 (year 1 10,000 × 1.1, year 2 11,000 × 1.1, year 3 12,100 × 1.1 = 13,310)

96 C, 40 (500 cl = 5 l, 200 divided by 5 = 40)

97 C, 9% (180/2,000 × 100 = 9)

98 C, 441 m^2 (216 + 225 = 441)

99 D, 1,800 m^3 (25 × 12 = 300 × 6)

100 E, 21 (462/22 = 21)

101 A, £5,000 (profit from A = £12,000 × 25% = £3,000, £2,000 × 40% of £5,000)

102 B, £960 (loses £480 a year × 3 = £1,440; deduct this from the original cost)

103 A, 4 to 1 (365 − 73 = 292 days it will not rain, on 73 it will, therefore odds of 292:73 which simplifies to 4:1)

104 C, 3/4 (1− $(1/2)^2$ = 3/4)

105 A, 1/4 (1/2 × 1/2 = 1/4)

106 C, 7/8 (this is an analogous question to asking, 'What is the probably of getting all tails?', 1/2 × 1/2 × 1/2 = 1/8, only here we want the opposite, ie this not happening, therefore 1 − 1/8 = 7/8)

107 C, 1/8 (answer, 1/2 × 1/2 × 1/2 = 1/8, same as all of them are tails)

108 D, $X = 1$ ($1^2 + 1 = 2$, $Y_2 = 2$)

109 B, for all $X < -1$

Chapter 4 Data interpretation

1 A – 3 for a win, B – 1 for a draw and C – 0 for a loss
Team F has scored no points from three losses – proving that a loss scores no points. Team E has scored only one point from one draw and two losses – proving that a draw must be worth one point. Team B, with one loss and three wins, has nine points so a win must be worth three.

2 D, 11 games
There are many ways of working this out – one of the simplest is to add up the total number of wins, draws and losses and divide by two.

3 A, 4
Each team must play 5 games. With two teams playing each game there must be 15 games in total, so with 11 played there must be four remaining.

4 B, 2
With teams A and B both with one match to play and three points available for a win, either team can win.

5 B, 2
Congratulate yourself if you got this right because these questions don't get more difficult than this. So far, E must have drawn with A and lost the other games. F has only played winning teams. Therefore E and F have not yet played each other. One of the remaining games must be E vs F. They cannot both accumulate sufficient points to be level with C and D.

6 E, 44

32 points have already been won. If none of the remaining games are draws then an additional 12 points will be won, giving a total of 44.

7 a. November had the highest level of rainfall;

b. September had the lowest.

8 A, November

The increase from 1.1 inches of rainfall to 2.4 inches of rainfall is the greatest increase.

9 D, February

The decrease from 2.1 inches of rainfall to 1.2 inches of rainfall is the greatest.

10 D, May

The increase from 0.8 inches of rainfall to 1.0 inches of rainfall is the lowest increase.

11 B, 14.4 inches. The graph is too small to calculate the exact quantities but by estimating them you can identify B as the only suggested answer close to the estimated value.

12 A, February

With 1.2 inches of rain, February exactly represented the average rainfall for the year.

13 a. Other; b. Council Tax

These are the largest and smallest segments of the chart.

14 C, 25%

C is exactly one-quarter of the chart – therefore 25% of expenditure.

15 E, £360

25% of £1,440 = £360

16 D, £480

If 25% of £480 is paid in tax, £360 will remain to pay the rent.

17 D, £28,800

If 20% of all after-tax income is saved, then rent equates to 25% of 80% of after-tax income. Therefore rent at £360 per month represents 25% × 0.8 = 20% of after-tax income. Therefore after-tax income = £360 × 5 = £1,800. With tax at 25% then monthly income before tax must be £2,400 and so annual income must be £2,400 × 12 = £28,800.

18   E, £4,320

If the household earns £28,800 before tax, then it will earn £28,800 × 0.75 after tax = £21,600. If 20% is saved then the total saved is £21,600 × 0.2 = £4,320.

19   A, zero

20   B, linear

21   C, exponential

22   B, linear

23   C, exponential

24   vii, $P = 0$

25   ii, $P = h$

26   vi, $P[i] = P[i - 1] + h$

27   i, $P = 2h$ and iv, $P = h \times 2$

28   iii, $P = h^2$

29   A, 1

The population of culture A appears to remain static, not varying over time.

30   C, 400

The growth of culture D is linear, with the population equivalent to twice the elapsed hours.

31   B (look for key points, such as the value of x when $y = 0$)

32   E, −5

33   A

34   A, 0

35   A

36   E, 4.5 and −4.5

37   B

38   C

39   A

40   D

41   A, True

42   A, True (employment in these sectors has the three highest values)

43   A, True

44   B, False (the value of the manufacturing GDP is 30 so there are more than five prime numbers, eg 5, 7, 17, 19, 23, 29)

45   B, False

46 A, True

47 C, Cannot tell (the information given does not include an explanation of how the data was calculated so the statement cannot be judged as either true or false)

48 A, True

49 A, True (respondents were asked about seven subjects and the median result of respondents who found the information about right was 67.4%, giving a shortfall against the target of 75%)

50 B, False (the figures are percentages and do not relate to the number of respondents)

51 B, 33.3 miles

20 min = 1/3 h; 1/3 × 100 = 33.3 miles

52 B, 1h 20 min

30 miles/h gives 0.5 miles/min, 40 miles takes 80 min as 40 × 0.5 = 80 min = 1 h 20 min

53 C, 25 miles

After 30 min the car has travelled 50 miles and the sports car 75 miles. 75 − 50 = 25 miles

54 A (speed 3.5)

55 C (speed 2)

56 C (acceleration = 0)

57 4

58 B, $Y = X + 1$

59 B, 0.0625 $((-1/4)^2 = 1/16 = 0.0625)$

60 C, 2 (2 × 2 = 4, 4/2 = 2)

61 C, $Y = X^2$

62 C, 90%

63 A, True

64 C, 17th

65 E, 27th

66 B, 11th (this is the date that most flights were delayed both arriving and departing)

67 B (on average, a higher percentage of both departures and arrivals are on time during this period)

68 a. Africa; b. Europe

69 Seven decades (North American population increased from 100 million in 1900 to 200 million in 1970)

70 Eight decades (African population increased from 200 million in 1900 to 600 million in 1980)

71 Decrease (even though the population increases overall, the rate of growth decreases – in other words, the growth in population is less than the growth of population during the 1950s)

72 Europe (the percentage growth in population is lowest in Europe)

73 A

74 a. Between 9 am and 10 am; b. Between 12 am and 1 pm

75 Gain (the value of the share was higher at 5 pm than at 8 am)

76 Between 9 am and 10 am

77 Between 12 am and 1 pm

78 The first four hours of the day

79 Buy at 10 am, sell at 4 pm

80 Cable/Satellite Television has gained 5% market share

81 Public Access Television has lost 6% market share

82 Internet (has increased from 1% to 5% – a 400% increase)

83 Newspapers (has fallen from 40% to 38% – a 5% decrease)

84 A, 1.0% (decreases from 41% to 40% – a decrease of 1%)

85 D, 25% (increase from 1% to 5% = ×5 so 5 × 5% = 25%)

86 a. A, January; b. C, September

87 D, June

88 C, June & July

89 E, September

90 D, 2.3

91 C, 3.2

92 B, £7 billion

93 B, £1 billion

94 B, 4%

95 C, £75 billion (monthly borrowing is £6.25 billion at 7.5%. £6.25 billion × 12 = £75 billion)

96 D, £81 billion (the average interest rate throughout the year is 6.5%, which equates to £6.75 billion average borrowing per month × 12 = £81 billion)

97 B, inversely proportional (as interest rates increase, borrowing decreases)

Chapter 5 Business judgement

Business judgement

Business comprehension

1 D, Shares
2 D, Revenue
3 A, Fixed-income securities
4 B, Earnings
5 C, Purchase
6 A, Input
7 D, Balance
8 D, Increase in price levels
9 C, A few firms in the market
10 A, Staff

Basic finance

11 D, £125,000 (50,000 + 75,000 = 125,000)
12 C, £2,175,000 (500,000 + 550,000 + 525,000 + 600,000 = 2,175,000)
13 A, 11% (total of misc. income (275) divided by [total of misc. income (275) + sales (2175) = 2450] = 0.11 or 11%)
14 B, 25 × 12 = 300, 35 × 12 = 420
15 A, 60–80% (£20 per month gives a price of £240 per year for the US user, which gives a difference of 240/420 = 60% and 240/300 = 80%)
16 C, 7,300,000 (20,000 × 365 = 7,300,000)
17 A, 6,666 h (20,000 × 20 = 400,000 minutes, 400,000 min/60 = 6,666 h)
18 C, 4%
19 A, £590 million (X × 1.10 = 650, 650/1.10 = 590)
20 B, £487.5 million (650 × 0.75 = 487.5)
21 B (adding up tons produced/year for all four factories = 189.5, adding up tons sold/year = 154, the difference is 35.5 tons)
22 C (Factory C has a 100% export ratio)
23 D, 50/80 = 62.5%

24   FDB represents the largest part of the chart
25   Samkob and Other
26   B, as Dansk Supermarked represents 20% of the market
27   A, as Samkob, Aldi and Other together represent exactly 25% of the market
28   D, as FDB represents 40% which equals 1,400 stores
29   B, as the three largest groups represent 75% of the market and therefore 2,625 stores

Business comprehension

30   A, True
31   C, Cannot tell
32   C, Cannot tell (we only know that the shares have not been this low for two years and do not know the price at which they traded three years ago)
33   B, False (price was $33.65)
34   C, Cannot tell
35   C, Cannot tell
36   A, True
37   A, True
38   C, Cannot tell
39   A, True
40   C, Cannot tell (the Australian dollar may momentarily have been stronger three years ago)
41   B, False
42   C, Cannot tell
43   C, Cannot tell
44   C, Cannot tell (we know that 31% of Belgium's beer production was exported but not what percentage of Belgium's GDP was beer)

Business judgement

45   P1 & Q3
46   E, Q5–Q2
47   B, Q2
48   A, P1

49   C, Q3

50   C, 70 units (you can simply read off the graph that at £8 per unit the output will equal 70)

51   A, £6/unit (at quantity 70, the average cost curve is at a price of 6)

52   B, £140 (a slightly harder question: profit per unit = MC − AC = 8 − 6 = 2. At a production of 70 units this gives a profit of 70 × 2 = 140)

53   B, 40 units will be produced and the firm is now making a loss as AC is higher than MC at an output of 40

54   C, discount coupons (we are told that the buy decision is made in market A almost entirely on price therefore of the suggested answers, offering discount coupons in this market is most likely to produce an increase in sales)

55   B, staff costs and building rent (a fixed cost does not change with the level of production and costs such as raw materials used and utility bills do increase with production. It might be argued that staff costs increase with production but traditionally staff costs are treated as a fixed cost)

56   B (in terms of value of sales it is clear that market B is a much smaller market than market A, and therefore may well be best suited for niche marketing techniques)

57   C, in an awareness survey women were found to be three times more aware of the Royal Tea brand than men (all the suggested answers to some extent support the assumption but suggested answer C best supports it. By definition customers have greatest brand awareness and suggested answer C best supports the assumption because it specifically investigates the question of brand awareness and gender, and it identifies a significant factor – women are 3× more aware than men – that supports the assumption that most customers are women. Suggested answer D is only concerned with market B)

58   A (one of the market research findings regarding market B is that Customers perceive higher price to imply higher quality and for this reason we can infer that by lowering the price we risk undermining the customer perception of quality, and this would not help sales)

59 C, competitor brands are winning Royal Tea's market share (the sales of Royal Tea in market A have remained relatively consistent – but for the exception of 2006 – and so do not support the finding that competitor brands are winning Royal Tea's market)

60 D, recruit more sales representatives (a push strategy in sales involves activities that 'push' a product into a market. Only suggested answer D is an example of a push strategy; all the others are pull strategies that aim to increase customer demand and 'pull' the product into the market and thereby increase sales)

Chapter 6 Data sufficiency

1 C, Cannot tell
2 B, False
3 C, Cannot tell
4 A, True
5 C, Cannot tell
6 A, True
7 B, False
8 C, Cannot tell
9 C, Cannot tell
10 B, False
11 A, True
12 C, Cannot tell
13 A, True
14 C, Cannot tell
15 B, False
16 C, Cannot tell
17 B, False
18 C, Cannot tell (the passage does not comment on whether or not the BTA believes the number of tourists will decrease)
19 A, True
20 B, False

21   A, True (6 lbs × 2 × 2 × 2 × 2 × 2 × 2 × 2 × 2 × 2 × 2 = 12,280 lbs = 877.7 stone on day 11, compared with 18 × 40 = 720 stone which is the total weight of the elephants)

22   A, True (divide the hexagon into equal triangles and count those inside and outside the triangle)

23   B, False (the athlete averages 15 mph (30 minutes at 20 mph and 30 minutes at 10 mph). The total time taken is 1 hour, so the athlete must travel 15 miles)

24   A, True, 7.07 miles (ie the square root of 50 = 5^2 + 5^2. The yacht has sailed along the short sides of an isosceles, right-angle triangle so Pythagorean theorem applies)

25   B, False (it would beat 31,536,000 times. Once per second × 60 = 60 times per minute × 60 = 3,600 times per hour × 24 = 86,400 times per day × 365 = 31,536,000 times per year)

26   C, Cannot tell (without knowing the fuel economy of the car it is not possible to calculate how far the car will travel on a tank of petrol)

27   B, False (25 words × 60 minutes = 1,500 words. It would take four hours at this speed)

28   A, True (15/3 × 25 = 125)

29   A, True (the sum of the angles of any triangle is 180 degrees, whilst the sum of the angles of a square is 360 degrees)

30   A, True (the total payable on a £500 loan at an APR of 20% would be £550 as the interest is constantly reducing as the loan is repaid. Paying £50 for 12 months totals £600 and so is more expensive)

31   B, False (the car will have averaged a speed of 30 mph and so will have travelled only 30 miles)

32   A, True (the car will have averaged a speed of 60 mph and so will have travelled 120 miles)

33   B, False (the value of the savings will depreciate by the difference between the rate of inflation less the rate of interest. The money borrowed will depreciate at the full rate of inflation)

34   A, True (16% of £500,000 is £80,000 – covering the business costs)

35   C, Cannot tell (the return on the investment would depend on the value on the variable Bank of England base rate)

36   B, False

37   A, True (imagine a box drawn around the triangles. The volume of the box would be $2x^2$. The triangles would occupy exactly half the box so their combined area would be x^2)

38   A, True (discrete variables are distinct units on the range)

39   A, True (continuous variable data can be given a value at any point on the range)

40   B, False (the symbol represents the sum of values for x and is one of the basic terms in statistics so should be familiar)

41   A, True (this is a common function on any scientific calculator and one of the essential symbols in statistics)

42   D, None of these (you could say all of them but in data analysis average is considered an imprecise term. Instead use mean, mode or median, whichever is the more appropriate to the given situation)

43   B, False (multipliers can give rise to both increases and decreases)

44   A, True

45   A, True

46   B, False (the two statistical terms, independent (events) and mutually exclusive (events), have been interchanged to create the false statement. Change them back and you get the true statements. Events are independent if the outcomes have no effect on each other. Mutually exclusive events cannot happen at the same time)

47   A, True (all numbers have factors in that they are divisible by 1 and themselves)

48   A, True

49   B, False (the first two statements are incorrect, the third is correct)

50   B, False (the first and third statements are true and the second statement is false. A range contains four quartiles)

51   A, True

52   B, False (the first statement is correct but when a positive skew occurs the mean exceeds the median and when a negative skew occurs the mean is less than the median)

53 B, False (probability and possibility are not interchangeable terms although often confused)

54 C, Cannot tell

55 A, True

56 A, True

57 C, Cannot tell (we are only told that the UK economy has been outperforming the other major economies)

58 C, Cannot tell (you should only refer to the information given in the passage. The definition of recession given in the previous passage would allow you to identify the question as true but you have to be careful not to do this)

59 A, True (even though the UK economy is said to be the fastest growing of the G7 the rate of growth has still slowed from 2.9% to 2.3%)

60 C, Cannot tell (the passage does not state whether the UK economy grew or contracted during previous recessions)

61 C, Cannot tell

62 A, True

63 B, False

64 H

65 F

66 D

67 B (14 passengers at 45p would be more than £6)

68 A (14 passengers at 25p would be less than £4)

69 D (there are only 14 passengers on the bus to start with – if 8 have already left then no more than 6 can leave after them)

70 C (8 passengers leaving at the last stop would be more than £6)

71 C (in (1) and (2) together)

72 A (in (1) but not in (2))

73 E (in none of the statements)

74 B (in (2) but not in (1))

75 E (in none of the statements)

76 A (in (1) but not in (2))

77 E (in none of the statements)

78 E (in none of the statements)

79 C (in (1) and (2) together)

80   D (in (1) and (2) separately)
81   E (in none of the statements) – you still need the numerical value of Y to determine X
82   E (in none of the statements)
83   A (in (1) but not in (2))
84   B (in (2) but not in (1))
85   D (in (1) and (2) separately)
86   E (in none of the statements)
87   B (in (2) but not in (1))
88   C (in (1) and (2) together)
89   B (in (2) but not in (1))
90   D (in (1) and (2) separately)

Chapter 7 Mock test 1

Data interpretation

1   A (can clearly be seen from the table)
2   C (can clearly be seen from the table)
3   D (500 (demand at 8p) – 350 (demand at 12p) = 150 tonnes; decrease rather than increase because as price rises, demand decreases)
4   C (the price where the quantity demanded equals the quantity supplied; the price where there is no shortage or surplus)
5   A (500 (demand at 8p) – 200 (supply at 8p) = 300; shortage for the price is below the equilibrium price of 12p)
6   D (surplus created at 16p = 530 – 200 = 330 tonnes. Surplus created at 20p = 700 – 100 = 600 tonnes. Therefore, surplus will increase by 270 tonnes)
7   B (as is clearly illustrated from the UK's first bar in the graph)
8   A (as the graph clearly shows that Japan has the highest second bar (approximately 11%))
9   D (West Germany is the only country to experience this drop in average growth rate; 8% for 1953–58, whereas 6% for 1958–63)
10   D (as the graph clearly shows; approximately 7% for 1953–58, whereas approximately 11% for 1958–63 (4% increase))

11 D (as in all three years the fourth quarter has the highest sales revenue (283, 288 and 290 for 1992, 1993 and 1994 respectively))

12 C (137 is the lowest sales revenue during 1993)

13 A ((264 + 227 + 141 + 290)/4 = 230.5)

14 A (in 1992 the company has the largest difference between highest and lowest values; 153 compared to 151 and 149 in 1993 and 1994 respectively)

15 A (put in ascending order = 130, 220, 256, 283; therefore (220 + 256)/2 = 238 is the median for 1992)

16 B (1272/12 = 106 mm)

17 B ((24 hours/1 day) × 6 days = 144 hours; therefore, having 145 hours of sunshine, October is the correct answer)

18 B ((16 – 20)/20 = –0.2; therefore, decrease of 20%)

19 A (July has 230 hours of sunshine and four times less would be 57.5 hours; therefore, having only 56 hours of sunshine, January is the correct answer)

20 B (12,500 minutes × (1 hour/60 minutes) = 208.3 hours; only July and August have over 208.3 hours of sunshine)

21 C (average # of students per ins. = (total # of st./total # of ins.); Moldova = (3900/39) = 100 students)

22 D (currently, there are approximately 185 students per institution. In order to have the 'ideal' institutions with 100 students each, there must be a total of 13 institutions (1300/13 = 100). Therefore, 13 – 7 = 6 new institutions are needed)

23 D (Slovenia's annual fees range between $2,340 and $7,020 ($4,680). This is the biggest range between these countries; Hungary would be second with a range of $4,000)

24 D (despite the fact that the annual fees in Romania are low ($210). There is a very high number of students (130,100). Therefore, their government will be receiving: $210 × 130,100 = 27,321,000)

25 B ($ per institution = (# of students × annual fee)/# of institutions; [28,000 * ((4,800 + 800)/2)]/32 = $2,450,000)

26 A (6% rise in fees will result in fees costing $1,113 and number of students dropping to 14,308. Before the 6% rise, institutions are receiving: 1,050 × 14,600 = $15,330,000. After the 6%

rise, institutions are receiving: $1,113 \times 14,308 = \$15,924,804$. Therefore 6% rise causes institutions to *gain*: $15,924,804 - 15,330,000 = \$594,804$)

27   A (the first bar indicates that the 1998 GDP increased 4% on the previous period (ie 1997))

28   B (the second bar indicates that there was a 3% drop on the previous period (1998). Therefore, the GDP of 1998 ($500 million) became $485 million $(500 - (500 \times 0.03))$))

29   B (the graph clearly indicates that in year 7 there was a peak in both exports and investments in China)

30   D (despite the fact that Country X experienced the greatest increase in GNP in Year 2 (6% increase), the GNP continued increasing in Years 3 and 4. Therefore, Country X's GNP was highest in Year 4)

Mock test 2

Business judgement

1   A (employee insurance)

2   C (exchange rate)

3   B (equity)

4   A (dividends)

5   D (face value)

6   C (cash flow)

7   B (period to which they relate)

8   A (balance sheet)

9   B (opportunity cost of being in business)

10   A (bank loan)

11   Professional fees (total expenditure for salaries is £6,600 whereas for professional services it is £9,800)

12   25% $((1000 - 800)/800 = 0.25 = 25\%)$

13   Decrease (% increase in September–October's salaries = $(1200 - 1000)/1000 = 0.20 = 20\%$. Since August–September's increase was 25%, September–October's percentage increase has actually decreased in comparison (ie 25% to 20%))

14 £330 (of National Insurance total of £6,600. Therefore, NI = 6,600 × (0.05) = £330)

15 March (sales double in March ($2,000) compared to previous month of February ($1,000))

16 $10,000 (Director's loans + Other loans = Total income (in Jan). Therefore, 90,000 – 80,000 = $10,000)

17 $74,500 (Costs of sales + Administration costs + Other expenditure = Total costs. 13,600 + 27,100 + 33,800 = $74,500)

18 Month 6 (Gross profit = Sales – Cost of sales. Month 2 = 20,000 – 13,600 = $6,400. Month 4 = 40,000 – 27,200 = $12,800. Month 6 = 50,000 – 33,900 = $16,100)

19 Month 2 (Operating costs = Administration costs + Other expenditure. Month 1 = $38,300. Month 2 = $60,900. Month 3 = $52,300. Month 4 = $45,600. Month 5 = $44,900. Month 6 = $47,800)

Business comprehension

20 B (false)

21 A (declined)

22 B (£100.90)

23 B (false)

24 C ($55/(1.65)^2$)

25 D (11,960,000)

26 A (more than doubled)

27 A (true)

28 A (true)

29 C (cannot tell)

30 C (1,500,000)

31 B (false)

32 B (against the euro)

33 B (false)

34 C (cannot tell)

Business finance

35 B, Money firm is owed ('Debtors' indicates the money that should be received by its debtors. Cash has not been received this year, but it is accounted for in the balance sheet)

36 C, £94,340 (in order to calculate total fixed assets without depreciation, you add back depreciation (for it is negative, indicated by the fact that it is in parenthesis) to the total fixed assets. Therefore: TFA + Depreciation = 81,500 + 12,840 = 94,340)

37 D (since total fixed assets are four times total current assets, their ratio is 4:1 (ie 81,500:20,375 = 4:1))

38 D, Stocks (by multiplying the value of 'Miscellaneous' (375) by 16, it is possible to determine that it is the value of 'Stocks'. 375 * 16 = 6,000)

39 A, Bank loan (current liabilities represent payments that the firm will have to make within one year. Therefore, the only plausible answer is the bank loan)

Mock test 3

Business judgement

1 By subtracting total expenditure from total income

2 5,985 (can be found in the total expenditure (row B) under May)

3 The last cell of Row C and D (ie 'Monthly + or –' and 'Cash flow'). They are always equal, if the cash flow is calculated correctly

4 A, Drops by 12.5% ((1,400 – 1,600)/1,600 = –0.125 = –12.5%)

5 C, 3% (Transport costs/Total expenditure = 200/6,600 = 0.030303... = 3%)

6 C (aps = Savings/Income January = 100/1,000 = 0.1)

7 D, six (aps is approximately 0.09 for every month except January (6 months in total))

8 D (mps = $\Delta S/\Delta Y$ 0.2 = S/400. Therefore, savings will be increased by £80)

9 B (if Nike shoes are heavily advertised, demand is likely to rise; instead the decrease in price of Nike shoes will only result in a movement along the demand curve (D))

10 A (price elasticity of demand = (% QD)/(% P)Nike shoes = (0.25)/(0.5) = –0.5. Since demand curves are generally downward sloping, elasticity of demand will generally be a negative figure)

11 B (it is inelastic because the value is less than one, indicating that a change in price causes a proportionately smaller change in the quantity demanded)

12 B, Y_2 (equilibrium national income is where withdrawals equal injections)

13 C (multiplier is the number of times by which a rise in national income exceeds the rise in injections that caused it: Multiplier = $\Delta Y /\Delta J$. Country X = (200 – 150)/(20 – 10) = 50/10 = 5)

Mock test 4

Data sufficiency

Part 1

1 D, No further information is needed (slope of a line (M) = $(y_1 - y_2)/(x_1 - x_2)$. Given that the line passes through the origin, the coordinates of point B are not needed in order to calculate the slope. M = (6 – 0)/(3 – 0) = 6/3 = 2)

2 B, Day of the week (number of men – revenue is calculated by multiplying P * Q; therefore, if you are given the number of men present that night, knowing the day of the week under consideration (ie number of total people present), you can determine the number of women present that night. With this information, you can then calculate the revenue for that night. C and D give unnecessary information, for the women's entrance price is given in the passage and costs are not needed when calculating revenue)

3 A (this would confirm that § represents only the addition sign. $0 + 1 = 1, 0 - 1 = -1, 0 * 1 = 0, 0/1 = 0$. Therefore, it would then be possible to calculate 4 § 2. Knowing it is an addition sign, the result is 6. The other two equations do not establish § as being a precise sign. For B it could be either addition or subtraction, and for C it could be either multiplication or division)

4 B only. A is the definition of an isosceles triangle.

5 B, C & D (B provides the following formula: sp − (0.05 * sp) = 76,000. Therefore, it is possible to solve for sp. selling price (sp) = 80,000. C provides the following formula: sp = 150% (44,000). Therefore, it is possible to solve for sp. selling price (sp) = 66,000. D provides the following information: Andy's earnings = $10,000 \times 2 = 20,000$ sp (0.05) = 20,000. Therefore, it is possible to solve for sp. selling price (sp) = 400,000)

6 A and B (in order to calculate the area: A, B and C are needed. Given A and B, we can first calculate A and then use this to calculate C (the missing variable). Calculate A, using the sine rule: A/Sin A = B/Sin B (we know B = 90° and are given A and B). Then, knowing A and that A + B + C = 180, it is possible to calculate C. This will result in us knowing all three of the variables necessary for calculating the area: A, B, and C. Given B and C, we can calculate C directly. Calculate C, using the sine rule: C/Sin C = B/Sin B (we know B = 90° and are given B and C). However, we are still missing A in order to calculate the area. Therefore, calculate A, using the cosine rule: $a^2 = b^2 + c^2 - 2bc \cos A$ (we are given B and C and A can be found since we now know B as well as C). This will again result in us knowing all three of the variables necessary for calculating the area: A, B and C)

7 B (circle's diameter − circle's circumference = 2r and Area = r^2. Therefore, with the diameter, it is possible to calculate the circle's radius (r) and consequently calculate both circumference and area)

8 D, None (compound interest is calculated as follows: $A = P (1 + r/100)^n$, where A = amount (final sum in the investment); P = principal (starting sum); r = percentage rate; n = time period. Therefore, since P, r and n are given in the passage, no further information is needed)

9   C, Value of f (the word *and* means intersection between bus and train, and is depicted by the area $e + f$. However, e represents the number of people that use the car as well as the bus and train. Since the question asks for bus and train *only*, the answer is f, the intersection of bus and train users and none other)

10   A and C (the word *or* means union between car and train, and is depicted by the area $a + b + c + d + e + f$. Therefore, we need to know both the number of people that use the car (X) as well as the number of people that use the train (Y), in order to calculate the number of people that use the car *or* the train (ie # of car users + # of train users = $X + Y$). A gives us the value of $X + Y$ directly, if we plug Z into the formula: $X + Y = 40,000$. C gives us the value of X and Y individually: $X = 25,000$ and $Y = 3(25,000) = 75,000$. Therefore, we can calculate that $X + Y = 100,000$)

11   A, B, and C (knowing Mary's height alone, it is possible to calculate Ben's (Mary = 2 Ben). Then with Ben's height, it is possible to calculate Jack's height (Ben = 3 Jack). Knowing Ben's height, it is possible to calculate Jack's height directly (Ben = 3 Jack). Similarly to A, knowing David's height alone, it is possible to calculate Jack's height. This is because David and Mary have the same height; therefore, with Mary's height it is possible to find Ben's and consequently Jack's)

12   C (the only *extra* information which the student needs before making a decision is the probability of passing the Biology final exam. The probability of passing the Chemistry final exam (b) is given in the passage (1 in 20 = 5%) and the probability of failing the Chemistry final exam (a) is not needed (even if it was needed, it could be calculated from the passage = 95%). Therefore, the only correct answer would be C. With this information, the student could evaluate which science class is easier)

13   A, B and D (the range, mode and median can be calculated without knowing the exact value of x. Only the mean requires the x value to be explicitly given. A – The range is the difference between the highest and lowest values in a distribution; therefore, it would be $12 - 2 = 10$ regardless of x's value for it is less than 12. B – The mode is the value that occurs most often; therefore, it would be 2 regardless of x's value. x is between 8 and 12 and thus there is no possibility of it being like a number already given in the set of data. D – The median is the middle value when the data has been arranged in order of size; therefore, in 2, 2, 4, 8, x, 12, it would be $(8 + 4)/2 = 6$. Since x is definitely greater than 8, its value does not need to be known when calculating the median of this set of data)

14   A, B and C (only the quantity of potatoes consumed in 1992 (ie current quantities (z) is not needed). This is because the base-weighted price index is calculated as follows: $\Sigma p_n q_0 / \Sigma p_0 q_0$. A – w is needed in order to calculate p_0 (ie base-year price), which is needed. B – x is needed in order to calculate q_0 (ie base-year quantity), which is needed. C – y is needed in order to calculate p_n (ie current price), which is needed)

15   D (in order to calculate the standard deviation of a set of data, we need the value of x, the mean of x (ie $\bar{x}$), and the number of items in the set of data)

16   B, C and D (these statements are all true. There is sufficient data provided in B, C and D, but not in A.

B – Given that P (A) = ¼ and that P (B) = ½, it is possible to calculate P (A and B). P (A and B) = P (A) * P (B) = 0.125).

C – Given that P (A or B) = ¾, we know that P (A) + P (B) = ¾. Therefore, knowing P (A) = ¼, it is possible to calculate P (B).

¼ + P (B) = ¾
P (B) = ¾ – ¼
P (B) = ½

Hence, now knowing both P (A) = ¼ and P (B) = ½, it is possible to calculate P (A and B). P (A and B) = P (A) * P (B) = 0.125.

D – Given that P (B) = ½ and that P (A) / P (B) = ½, it is possible to calculate P (A).

$$P(A) / P(B) = \frac{1}{2}$$
$$P(A) / \frac{1}{2} = \frac{1}{2}$$
$$P(A) = \frac{1}{2} * \frac{1}{2}$$
$$P(A) = \frac{1}{4} = 0.25$$

Therefore, now knowing both $P(A) = \frac{1}{4}$ and $P(B) = \frac{1}{2}$, it is possible to calculate $P(A \text{ and } B)$. $P(A \text{ and } B) = P(A) * P(B) = 0.125)$

Part 2

17	A, True
18	C, Cannot tell
19	A, True
20	C, Cannot tell
21	B, False
22	C, Cannot tell
23	A, True
24	A, True
25	A, True
26	A, True
27	C, Cannot tell
28	C, Cannot tell
29	C, Cannot tell
30	A, True
31	A, True
32	A, True
33	B, False
34	B, False (accumulative interest would give a value more like 1.04% a month)